God's Holy Fire

A Theology of the Icon

Lawrence Cross

with

Andrew Quinlan, Joseph Leach,

Birute Arendarcikas rsm

and Brendan Cooke

Published in 2014 by

Freedom Publishing Company Pty Ltd
35 Whitehorse Rd, Balwyn, Melbourne, Victoria 3103, Australia

Telephone: (61 3) 9816 0820
Fax: (61 3) 9816 0899

Email: books@freedompublishing.com.au
Website: www.freedompublishing.com.au

Printer: Brougham Press
33 Scoresby Rd, Bayswater Victoria 3153, Australia

Cover design and layout: Manark Printing
28 Dingley Avenue, Dandenong, Victoria 3175

In the House of the Spirit:
A Western Christian's Guide to the Sacraments in the Byzantine Church

ISBN 978-0-9925406-0-9

CONTENTS

THE OLD TESTAMENT AND EARLY CHRISTIANITY

In many ways, both the history and the theology of Christianity would lead us to believe that it should stand alongside Judaism and Islam as a religion that is anti-image. How Christianity used images throughout its history and eventually (in Greek speaking Christianity at least) developed a theology and cult of image is a long and complex story. The question of images would be only of historical interest if it were not relevant to the life of the Church today. It is no exaggeration to say that religious art is in crisis. Artists still draw inspiration from religious themes, but the cultic use of images in private religious devotion and public worship is at a low point. Richard Harries points out how important it is for Christians to come to some understanding of the role of art in their religious life. He wrote:

> As with the experience of beauty in nature, unless the Christian faith has an understanding and place for the arts it will inevitably fail to win the allegiance of those for whom they are the most important aspect of life. For they will see in the Christian faith only what strikes them as flat, moralistic and platitudinous compared to the troubling, haunting depths of Mahler, or King Lear. Unless the experience of beauty in nature and the arts is encompassed and affirmed the Christian faith will seem to have nothing of interest and importance to say. This is not, however, just a tactic to win the allegiance of the lost. The fact is that God is beautiful and the Church is hiding this.[1]

In order to achieve a balanced approach to the question of the role of art, and images in particular, in the life of the Church, it is necessary to evaluate both the Church's past teaching and practice in this area. The theological battle over the place of images in the life of the Church seems to have erupted out of nowhere in 778 CE and to have troubled only the Greek-speaking side of Christianity. In fact, the debate was to last over one hundred years. In a strange parallel the debates concerning the Eucharist that raged in the Western Church from the Middle Ages onwards, never touched the Eastern Churches. For this reason, the Western Church has a much more precise way of speaking about the nature of the Eucharist than do the Eastern Churches. Correspondingly, the Greek Church (and those Churches that received their faith from her) have a much more complex and subtle approach to the question of images than western Christian Churches. Despite the role images in the Church played in the Protestant Reformation in the sixteenth century, neither those who were against images (Protestant) nor those who defended them (Roman Catholics) produced a true "theology" of religious art. Nevertheless, the opponents of images seem to have the authority of Scripture of their side. How could Christians ever justify something that is so clearly prohibited in the Old Testament? Jaroslav

---

[1]   Richard Harries, *Art and the Beauty of God: A Christian Understanding* (London: Mowbray, 1993), 5-6.

Pelikan sums up the dilemma as follows:

> Was prohibition of "graven images" part of what Christians
> could dismiss as the temporary ceremonial and political law
> obligatory only for the people of Israel (as the commandments
> requiring observance of Saturday as the Sabbath, kosher food,
> and circumcision were taken to be)? Or was the injunction
> against images meant in the Decalogue as part of the universal,
> natural law (as were the commandments prohibiting adultery,
> murder, and theft, received also by Paul (Rom. 13:9) and thus
> permanently binding not only upon the Jewish community under
> the old dispensation, but no less binding upon the Christian
> community even after it had been set free from the authority
> of the law of Moses as a whole - in fact permanently binding
> upon the entire human community simply of virtue of its being
> created.[2]

In many ways the contemporary Christian community is in a better position to
appreciate the development of the Old Testament theology of images than either
the eighth century iconoclasts or the controversialists of the sixteenth century
Reformation. However, we should keep in mind that when trying to understand
the Old Testament attitude to the use of images, the available evidence is not only
the written text, but also archaeological remains. There is widespread evidence that
by the beginning of the Christian era, Jews were decorating their synagogues with
figurative art. Because of the uniqueness of Israel's opposition to images of her
God, it is tempting to take the simplistic approach of believing that this opposition
was constant and unchanging. Reading the texts that deal with images, we can see
that the attitudes expressed during the long history of Israel were often unclear and
ambivalent. Throughout her history, Israel adopted a variety of attitudes to art both
secular and religious. It has to be remembered that the Jewish religious experience
was mainly "historical" rather than "philosophical". We look in vain for a reasoned
argument against artistic production and what we would call "idolatry". However,
there are many texts of the Old Testament, especially those of the Prophetic tradition
and the Deuteronomic reform, that speak about the evils of "idols". Nevertheless,
these texts usually represent a call to a general reform of the nation and a return to a
simpler and more primitive religious cult. The nearest that we get to an anti-image
"theology" is found Deuteronomy 4, 15-20:

> On the day when the Lord spoke to you out of the fire on Horeb,
> you saw no figure of any kind; so take good care not to fall
> into the degrading practice of making figures carved in relief,

---

[2]   Jaroslav Pelikan, *Imago Dei The Byzantine Apologia for Icons* (New Haven and London: Yale University Press,
      1990), 54.

in the form of a man or a woman, or of any animal on earth or bird that flies in the air, or of any reptile on the ground of fish in the waters under the earth. Nor must you rise your eyes to the heavens and look up to the sun, the moon, the stars, all the host of heaven, and be led on to bow down to them and worship them; the Lord your God assigned these for the worship of the various peoples under heaven.[3]

Israel cannot portray her God because God is not revealed through "figures" but rather through words. This is in opposition to traditional religious practice. As the Old Testament scholar Von Rad explains, image and revelation usually go hand in hand. He wrote:

What (image) speaks about is ...how the deity is pleased to reveal Himself, for the image is first and foremost the bearer of a revelation. Ancient peoples felt the divine powers to be very close to them. No doubt these came from below and were incalculable; but in cultic symbols and images they approached men in a way that was helpful. In terms of this belief, the whole world is like a curtain which permits the divine to be seen through it; or at least such a transparency was possible wherever the deity authorised something material as its manifestation.[4]

Nevertheless, the reason for Israel's rejection of images and idols is never fully explained in the Old Testament. It is not possible to attribute a greater level of religious sophistication to Israel than that of her neighbours. From numerous quotations found in the Old Testament, it is clear that the people of Israel conceived of God as having a concrete form like that of a human being. In Isaiah 30:27 ff, for example, the prophet writes:

See, the name of the Lord comes from afar,

his anger blazing and his doom heavy.

His lips are charged with wrath

and his tongue is a devouring fire...[5]

It is even more difficult to come to a simple understanding of Israel's attitude to images when we begin to examine the various cultic practices that are mentioned in the Old Testament. At the most extreme end of the scale is the story found in the book of Judges:

There was once a man named Micah from the hill-country

---

3   Deut 4:15-20.

4   Gerhard Von Rad, *Old Testament Theology*, vol. 1 (Edinburgh: Oliver and Boyd, 1962), 214.

5   Isa 30:27 ff.

of Ephrini. He said to his mother, "You remember the eleven hundred pieces of silver which were taken from you, and how you called down a curse on the thief in my hearing? I have the money; I took it and now I will give it back to you". His mother said, "May the Lord bless you, my son." So he gave the eleven hundred pieces of silver back to his mother, and she said, "I now solemnly dedicate this money of mine to the Lord for the benefit of my son, to make a carved idol and a cast image." He returned the money to his mother, and she took two hundred pieces of silver and handed them too a silversmith, who made them into an idol and an image which stood in Micah's house.[6]

This story may have been included to demonstrate the anarchy that reigned in Israel before the institution of the monarchy. However, the idol in the story is taken by all to be a representation of the God of Moses, and therefore shows the diversity of understanding that existed about the role of cultic images in Israel's religious life. At the very centre of Israel's religious life stands the temple, yet even here what seems to be the clear prohibition of images is ignored. The first book of Kings, chapters six and seven, give a detailed description of the Temple of Solomon. How accurate or anachronistic this description might be is not of interest here. What is clearly shown is that at some time the temple contained images of living beings.

I Kings 6:23 - 24, 29 reads:

In the inner shrine [Solomon] made two cherubim of wild olive, each ten cubits high. Each wing of the cherubim was five cubits long, and from wing-tip to wing-tip was ten cubits ... Round all the walls of the house he carved figures of cherubim, palm trees, and open flowers, both in the inner chamber and in the outer.[7]

The temple also contained a "Sea of cast metal"[8] which was supported by statues of twelve oxen.[9] Solomon is harshly criticised for allowing his many wives and concubines to corrupt the purity of Israel's religious life, but nowhere do we find a criticism of his disregard for the second commandment. When we turn to the extraordinary events of the reign of the seventh century King of Judah, Josiah, we see that Israel's capacity for religious syncretism was greater than any prophetic text would lead one to believe. In 2 Kings 23, we have the story of how the king cleansed the Temple of a variety of "pagan" idols, sacred symbols and even temple prostitutes. Nevertheless, the graven images placed in the Temple by Solomon were left intact. Away from the cult of the Temple we find that the prophetic movement

---

6   Judg 17:1-4.
7   I Kgs 6:23-24, 29.
8   1 Kgs 7:23.
9   1 Kgs 7:25.

displayed a less tolerant attitude to images. In the Book of Isaiah we read the following declaration by the imageless God of Israel:

> To whom will you liken me and make me equal, and compare me, that we may be alike? Those who lavish gold from the purses, and weigh out silver in the scales, hire a goldsmith, and he makes it into a god; then they fall down and worship! They lift it upon their shoulders, they carry it, they set it in its place, and it stands there; it cannot move from its place. If one cries to it, it does not answer or save him from trouble.[10]

In Chapter 44 the Prophet satirises the folly of idolatry by pointing out that the idol maker uses half his wood to make a god and the other half to cook his dinner. By the time of the writing of the Book of Daniel, the theme of the worship of images is the subject of comic satire. In the story of Bel and the Dragon, the Prophet reveals that the priests of Bel, along with wives and children, consume the food offered to the god.[11] What may have been a serious temptation for Israel (as outlined in Exodus 20) has now become the subject of humour and contempt.

What seems to emerge throughout the history of Israel is a polarity of attitude towards images that is related to an inner sense of national identity. At the time of Solomon it seems natural that the temple of the living God be adorned with the best that money could buy and art could fashion. This period represents the high point in the cult of the God of Israel. However, this time is followed by a period of moral and national degradation that eventually leads to exile and the destruction of the nation. During this period, the Prophetic movement calls for a return to the simple purity of the desert religion. The "return to the law" represented by the "Deuteronomic reforms" were so far-reaching that it seems that all representations of living beings, even on coins, seals and rings, were banned. In post-Exile Israel the economic and religious conditions did not encourage artistic production. However, the limited archaeological evidence available in the form of coins shows that the total ban on the representation of people and animals had been lifted. When Israel came within the influence of Greek culture (at a much earlier period than coming under political influence), both her economic and intellectual conditions changed radically. It was from this encounter that the decorative art of the first and second century synagogues was derived. If we ignore this development, it is impossible to reconcile the Old Testament ban on images so clearly given in Exodus, Deuteronomy and the Prophetic literature, with the archaeological evidence from various periods of Israel's history. In fact, it would seem that the Early Christians shared the same attitude as their Jewish contemporaries when it came to art.

---

[10] Isa 46:5-7.
[11] Dan 14.

How do the Fathers of the Church Draw on the Old Testament to Attack Images?

The Early Christians were not at home in their society. Every aspect of its life was tinged with pagan religious practice. However, it should be remembered that Jews had faced many of the same problems already. As well as that, pagan religious attitudes varied from the superstitions of the uneducated to the abstract speculations of the various philosophical movements of late antiquity. It is simplistic to think, then, that Christians' attitude to art would have been formed solely from a reading of the Ten Commandments, or as a total rejection of the Old Testament and a gradual capitulation to pagan values and customs. As has been pointed out, the Old Testament's own ambiguity, and pagan philosophy itself, had a long tradition of suspicion of the use of images. The situation of the Early Church also presents us with the problem found in Judaism, namely, a body of literature that seems to be anti-image while at the same time archaeological evidence showing that Christians did use art in a religious context. Such a contradiction makes it essential that we understand the circumstances in which the Early Church articulated her thinking about the role of image in religion.

The Early Church was not interested in producing systematic theology. The writings that come down to us from the first 300 years of Christian history show that the Church was engaged in a struggle for her very existence and devoted her intellectual energy to those aspects of her faith that most touched the lives of believers and their immediate relations with the non-Christian society in which they lived. It was necessary for Christians to explain to pagans that faith in Christ was rational and comparable with all that was best in pagan society. The group of Christian authors who undertook this work of defending and promoting Christianity are called the "Apologists". The work of these writers was directed at pagan readers and therefore it could not call either on the absolute authority of the Jewish scriptures, nor on a deep knowledge of the New Testament writings. The arguments in defence of Christianity had to be based on ideas and beliefs that were held by the pagans themselves. By the second century CE, pagan philosophical culture had a long tradition that stretched back to the philosophers Plato (427-347 BCE) and Aristotle (384-322 BCE). Greek philosophers had always shown a great interest in ethics and questions relating to the purpose of human life. The Stoic school (founded by Zeno of Citium at Athens in the fourth century BCE) emphasized the interior and moral nature of religious belief, rather than the exterior and cultic aspects. The most influential school of philosophical thought at the time of the Christian Apologists was the "Neo-Platonic" school. The Neo-Platonists sought to combine the rigor of philosophical enquiry and morality with a mystical vision of the hidden nature of God.

The main accusation made by pagans against Christians was that they were atheists.

As far as pagans could see, Christians denied the existence of the gods and had no cult (temple and sacrifice) of their own. In order to refute this accusation, Christians had to show that the cult of the pagans was useless and that the Christian cult was a spiritual and interior cult. Using arguments drawn from pagan philosophy, the Christian Apologists attempted to show that the force of tradition was on their side, and that the currant state of pagan religious practice represented a slide into superstition and moral degradation. Drawing on the argument of the Stoic school of philosophy, the Apologists argued that the essence of religious belief was interior and moral. This was an idea that is never made explicit in the Old Testament, and it is quite alien to the Jewish religious mentality which does not distinguish between exterior and interior. If the Stoics – and by association the Christians – are right, images and sacrifices are irrelevant both to God and to the believer. The second line of argument is taken from the Neo-Platonists.

CHAPTER TWO

THE IDEA OF IMAGE IN THE PATRISTIC CHURCH

T he idea that God is above our understanding, and therefore that we cannot form an image of our Creator, is both strong and attractive. Anachronistically we attribute this idea to the early stages of Israel's religious experience, and thus the ban on images in the Jewish cult is given as a simple explanation. It is a short step to claim that Christianity took over this "anti-image" stance from the Old Testament and only slowly, through the corrupting influence of Paganism, were images introduced into the Church. Although archaeological evidence shows that from very early days Christians used religious painting, it is even more important to grasp the fact that the notion of "image" was always central to Christian experience of God. The theological use of the idea of image from the earliest times of Christian reflection provided the tools that later defenders of Christian art would use to defend and promote the use of icons both in private and public devotion.

The idea of '"image" is tied to the teaching of the Church on the Trinitarian nature of God, Father, Son and Holy Spirit, to the nature of Salvation, and the death and resurrection of the Incarnate second person of the Trinity. After 2,000 years of Christian history, the uniqueness and importance of these "truths" of faith seem to have lost their centrality. However, if they are ignored, Christianity is robbed of its most radical and important contributions. As von Schonborn has written:

> ...this, from the beginning, was the faith and the experience of
> the Church: that the gift of the Holy Spirit, bestowed on the
> believer, is the gift of God himself, that communion with Christ
> is communion with God. The church Fathers of the fourth
> century express this in their own language when they say: the
> gift of salvation, coming to us from Christ in the Holy Spirit,
> makes us "godlike". Yet the Son and Spirit can make us godlike
> only if they themselves are God.[12]

What both the teaching on the Trinity and the Incarnation tell us is that God is not isolated from creation and creatures, and that the reason for our existence is to share intimately in the inner life of God, Father, Son and Holy Spirit. The relationship between God and creation is a relationship based on invitation. God reaches out and invites us to share in Divine love. Underpinning our knowledge that God reveals the inner life of the Trinity to us is the knowledge that comes from revelation in the Old Testament and from our own reason, knowing that God is totally other and transcends all the boundaries of creation, including our own capacity for understanding. The task of the theologian, (one who speaks about God)

---

[12]   Christoph Von. Schönborn, *God's Human Face: The Christ-Icon* (San Francisco: Ignatius Press, 1994), 26.

starting with St. Paul, has been to find words and categories that can communicate the Church's faith and lived experience of the Trinity and the Incarnation. In this task the concept of image is of the utmost importance.

Image in St Paul

In the thought of St. Paul we find the dual nature of the idea of image, both Trinitarian and Incarnational. Jesus is the "image" of the Father, and at the same time, humanity is created in the "image" of Christ. St. Paul uses the word 'image' to describe Jesus because, as a preacher of the Risen Lord, he must answer two questions; first "Who is Jesus Christ?" and second, "What is the goal of a human life in particular, and humanity in general?"

If we were to set about answering the question "Who is Jesus Christ?" we would probably feel that the answer lay in history. The task would be to collect as many historical "facts" about Jesus and then make an informed judgement. Consequently, it comes as a surprise to us that St. Paul says so little about the actual life of Jesus. For St. Paul, Jesus does not belong to the past, but is alive and active not only in the Church, but in the entire cosmos. In the Letter to the Colossians we read:

> [Jesus] is the image of the invisible God; he has primacy over all created things. In him everything in heaven and earth was created, not only visible but also the invisible orders of thrones, sovereignties, authorities, and powers: the whole has been created through him and for him.[13]

Throughout the Pauline Letters we find a variety of ways of expressing the relationship that exists between Jesus and the Father. All of these expressions recall the Gospel of John, where Jesus says: "He who has seen me has seen the Father"[14] and the more striking saying "I and the Father are one."[15] In the letter to the Hebrews we read that Jesus is like a mirror reflecting God's glory, and a being on which God's image is stamped clearly.[16] Again in Colossians we read, "In [Jesus] the whole fullness of the deity dwells bodily."[17] St. Paul is not trying to find a philosophical explanation for the relationship between Jesus and the Father, but rather he is attempting to describe what the faith of the Church is. However, he bequeathed a rich theological vocabulary to the Patristic Church. The use of the word "image" allows St. Paul to speak about the equality that exists between the Father and Jesus, while at the same time not attempting to answer the question of how the Father and the Son are one. The degree of equality that exists between the Father and Son will depend on our notion of the degree of equality that exists

---

[13]   Col 1:14-17.
[14]   John 14:9.
[15]   John10:30.
[16]   Heb 1:3.
[17]   Col 2:9.

between an image and the source of that image. This is a question that St. Paul never attempts to answer. The unique roles of Jesus as "Lord" and especially "Saviour" depend on the equality that He enjoys with the Father. In this way the Early church believed that when Jesus acted, it was God who acted.

On a second level, the idea of "image" provides St. Paul with a link that exists between Jesus and the whole of creation, but especially with the human race. From the book of Genesis, Judaism was already familiar with the idea that the human person was created in the image of God. We read in the Creation story:

> Then God said, "Let us make man in our own image, after our
> likeness. ... So God created man in his own image, in the image
> of God he created him; male and female he created them.[18]

It would seem that God intended humanity to be his representative on earth, that is, to be an image of the invisible ruler of the universe. As the story unfolds it becomes clear that through sin, the unique "likeness" to God was lost, but in the flow of later human history, the Father sends the Son to restore the divine image. As we read in the Letter to the Romans:

> Then as one man's trespass led to condemnation for all men,
> so one man's act of righteousness leads to acquittal and life
> for all men. For as by one man's disobedience many were
> made sinners, so by one man's obedience many will be made
> righteous.[19]

St Paul wrote to the Church in Corinth:

> The first man was from the earth, a man of dust; the second man
> is from heaven ... Just as we have borne the image of the man of
> dust, we shall also bear the image of the man of heaven.[20]

The moral and theological implications of the first and second Adam are pointed out to new Christians in the letter to the Ephesians:

> Put off your old nature which belongs to your former manner of
> life and is corrupt through deceitful lusts, and be renewed in the
> spirit of your minds and put on the new nature, created after the
> likeness of God in true righteousness and holiness.[21]

In this way, we become images of God in Jesus who is the perfect divine image.

---

[18]   Gen 1:26-27.
[19]   Rom 5:19.
[20]   1 Cor 15:47,49.
[21]   Eph 4:22-24.

Patristic Church

As the Church grew in both numbers and political and intellectual power, the question of the nature of Jesus Christ and his relationship to God the Father became ever more pressing. St. Paul provided an outline of salvation history, but he did not give the details. Numerous attempts were made to give a satisfactory explanation to the mystery of how the Father and the Son are one and yet two. The debate eventually split the Church and led to the calling of the first universal Church council in the city of Nicea (near present day Istanbul) in 325 CE. Although the council proclaimed that Jesus was truly human and truly divine, stating that He was "one in being" with the Father, the debate did not simply end there. Those who rejected the Council belonged to the Arian party, which took its name from an Egyptian theologian Arius (c. 250 - c. 336 CE) who taught that the Son was a "lesser" god, an instrument that the Father used first to create and then save humanity. Such a teaching appealed to the educated pagans of the time because it preserved God from any contact with the material world. Arius' teaching was based on reason and philosophical method, and therefore the faith of the Church – that contradicted this teaching – had to find expression in a reasonable and coherent way. The preaching of St. Paul had to be underpinned with the language of philosophy. The great champion of the Church against Arius was his fellow Egyptian St. Athanasius (296-373 CE). St. Athanasius spent most of his life in exile and "on the run" as the teaching of Arius had great appeal for the political powers of the 4th century. Nevertheless, St. Athanasius left a large body of writing that seeks to clarify the relationship and equality of the Son to the Father. In his approach to the question of the Trinity, he calls on St. Paul's notions of the Son as "image" of the Father. St. Athanasius wrote:

> ... let us consider the attributes of the Father, in order to see if the image truly represents him. The Father is eternal, immortal, powerful, radiant light, king, almighty God, Lord, creator, and sculptor. All this has to be present in the image as well, so that whoever has seen the Son has also seen the Father (Jn 14:19). If, however, this is not the case, but if on the contrary, as the Arians believe, the Son has come into existence and was not in existence from all eternity, then he is not the true image of the Father ...[22]

In order to make his point further, St. Athanasius uses the idea of the statue of the Emperor. These statues were very important in the fourth century CE and were found in almost every city of the Empire. They were regarded as representing the presence of the ruler among his people, somewhat in the way that man "represented" God on earth according to the creation story of Genesis. St. Athanasius points out that anyone who had seen the Emperor in person would also recognise his statue and vice-versa (anyone having seen the statue would recognise the Emperor). He writes:

---

[22] *Discourse 1 Against the Arians*, 6, 21.

> That the saying "whoever has seen the Son has seen the Father"...
> may become more clear and understandable through the image
> of the emperor. The image shows the form and features of the
> emperor, and the emperor shows the same form represented in
> the image. The image of the emperor shows exactly what he
> looks like, so that whoever later sees the emperor, will recognise
> the person he saw in the image. Since there exists a complete
> likeness, the image could say to the person who, after having
> gazed on the image, wants in addition to see the emperor
> himself: "I and the emperor are one; for I am in him and he is in
> me; and whatever you have seen in him you also see in me". He,
> therefore, who honours the image, also honours the emperor in
> it; for it contains his form and shows his features.[23]

The truth of St. Athanasius' statement is born out even today by the fact that if
someone wants to show disrespect to some prominent public figure, they often
deface a public image of that person. The belief that the Son is the "image" of the
Father helps St. Athanasius to explain the reason for the Incarnation; that is, why
the Son of God became human. St. Athanasius returns to the book of Genesis and
to the idea that we are created in the "image and likeness of God," and that through
sin this likeness is almost destroyed. In his work "On the Incarnation," he wrote:

> Just as when a figure which has been painted on wood is spoilt by
> dirt, it is necessary for him whose portrait it is to come again so
> that the picture can be renewed in the same material, for because
> of his portrait the material on which it is painted is not thrown
> away, but the portrait is redone on it, even so the all-Holy Son
> of the Father, who is the image of the Father, came to our world
> to renew humanity who had been made in his likeness, and, as
> one lost, to find him through forgiveness of sins.[24]

St. Athanasius has taken the language of Scripture firstly from St. Paul (who called
Jesus "The image of the invisible God") [25] to speak about the second person of
the Trinity, and then the words of Genesis "image and likeness" to explain the
relationship between the Incarnate second person and the human race. Nevertheless,
although St. Athanasius is convinced that there is a real, objective link between an
image and the "prototype" (the source of the image), he never provides an exact
description of what "becoming [the] flesh" of the image of God actually meant. If
Jesus is the image of the Father in human nature, does that mean that by looking
at the face of Jesus we actually see the face of God? How do these two realities,

---

[23]   *Discourse 3 Against the Arians*, 23, 5.

[24]   R.W.Thompson, trans., *De Incarnatione* ed. by R.W. Thompson (Oxford: Oxford University Press, 1971), no.14, 167.

[25]   Col 1:15.

human and divine, relate to each other in the one person? Every new generation of Christians finds a way to describe this mystery of faith, but the Patristic Church, over a period of four hundred years, developed a precise language based on Scripture and philosophy that has been the touchstone of Christology (the study of the person of Jesus Christ) ever since. To follow these developments in detail would lead us a long way from the study of icons, but it is essential to remember that the Church has always thought and talked about art in a theological way. Christian art cannot be separated from belief in Jesus. Through the centuries, long discussion and debate on how to express the mystery of the Incarnation of Jesus – the whole way of looking at the relationship between the spiritual and material aspects of Christianity – took shape. The humanity of Jesus was just as essential to his role as Saviour and revelation of the Father as his divinity. It was not necessary to strip Christ of his human nature so that his divine nature could be revealed. As one of the great teachers of the Patristic Church, Cyril of Alexandria (d. 444 CE), wrote:

> Nobody can see the divine essence (being) in itself, for it is entirely invisible and beyond comprehension and power of reasoning: it is known in itself only by itself. Christ expresses this very truth: "Nobody knows the Son except the Father; nobody knows the Father except the Son, and to whom the Son wishes to reveal him" (Mt 11:27). The only-begotten Son shows us the exceeding beauty of God the Father whose radiant image he himself represents. For this reason he says, "Whoever sees me, sees the Father" (Jn 14:9). True, we behold the Son above all with the eyes of our hearts, but also with our bodily eyes; for he has humbled himself and has descended among us, while at the same time dwelling in the form of God and equal to God the Father, because according to his nature he is born of the Father.[26]

As Christian art developed in a "practical way" and seemingly without any theology of art, it was in fact dependent on the theology of the Incarnation for its very existence. In a non-verbal way, the Church expressed her faith that God was with her. Christian artists could depict his birth, death and even resurrection not only symbolically, but also "realistically". If Jesus had been a "mere man" his actions and teachings would not have had eternal significance. If, on the other hand, Jesus had only "seemed" to be human, the actions of his human life would also lack any significance and be considered only a type of "play acting". Because Christology struggled so long and hard with the mystery of the Incarnation, Jesus true God and true man, Christianity was not an imageless and hyper-spiritualised religion. In the final stages of the Christological struggle in the seventh-eighth centuries, images in fact were to play a vital role in giving the final shape to the Church's teaching on the person of Jesus.

---

[26] *Commentary on Luke*, Sermon LX, 276.

CHAPTER THREE

EARLY CHRISTIAN ART: BETWEEN ARCHAEOLOGY AND LEGEND

Religious art, just as any form of artistic production, depends for its existence not only on the artist but also on the circumstances that permit the artist to work. The history of Christian art is tied to the history of the Church herself, and our knowledge of its origins and development can be no greater or lesser than our knowledge of the origins and development of the Early Church. Unfortunately for us, the first 200 years of Church history are not as well documented as later ages. We have the writings of the Apostolic Fathers (the half dozen or so letters and sermons produced in the late first century CE and early second century). We have the works of the Apologists from the middle and late second century. From these works we gain very little insight into the day-to-day life of the Early Christian. The second important factor in the life of the Early Christians was the constant threat of persecution. All this means that the origins of Christian art are not clear and are therefore open to a great deal of speculation. Nevertheless certain considerations must be keep in mind if we are to understand how and why Christian art could develop at all, and how the later and more sophisticated forms might find their origins in the first attempts to create a truly Christian art.

Considerations about the Formation of Christian Art.

The first consideration that we must make about Christian Art is its relationship to the Old Testament and the Jewish origins of Christianity. Given the strict prohibition on art found in the Old Testament (Ex 20:4-6, Ex 34:17), it would seem clear that Christianity represents a radical break with Jewish traditions. However, archaeological excavations in Palestine and especially in Syria have shown that third century CE Jews decorated their synagogues with painted scenes from the Old Testament. The best example of this is the synagogue at Dura Europus. This town, on an escarpment above the right bank of the Euphrates in present-day Syria, was on the frontier of the warring Roman and Persian Empires. It was taken by the Romans in 165 CE and then in 257 CE it fell to the Persians. Not long after, the town was abandoned and almost completely covered by sand. It was re-discovered in 1921. Scholars debate if the extensive artwork present in the synagogue of Dura is exceptional or not, but at the very least its existence shows that, contemporary with the Early Church, some elements of Judaism were open to the use of images.

A second consideration to be made is that Christianity did not "invent" any new art forms or styles. Art is to be considered as "Christian" art because of the content and purpose of the art and not because of its form or the methods used to produce it. Even if some elements of Judaism were happy to decorate their synagogues with images, these images were made in the style that was popular in the third and fourth century CE. The same must be said for the first example of Christian art that we have. These paintings, dating from around 200, reflect the style (and sometimes even the content) of contemporary pagan art.

A third consideration is the fact that Christians in the first 200 years of their existence were a marginalised group. The phenomenon that we call "persecution" is a very complex one and took a variety of forms, ranging from the local riot (like the anti-Jewish pogroms of Tsarist Russia) to a state organised attempt to eradicate Christianity from the whole Empire. Over almost 300 years of sporadic persecutions, there were periods of not only peace, but also tolerance. During these periods, Christians could meet in private houses given over for worship (the so-called house Churches), as well as construct their own burial places (the famous Catacombs). Nevertheless, the Community was always in danger of renewed hostility on a local and state level, so it difficult to know how many Christian artefacts were destroyed during the periods of anti-Christian violence. Also, even during peaceful times, the Church was never in a position of power so as to be able to build and decorate large public buildings. Therefore, any examples of Early Christian art would be private and the work of whatever artist the local community could provide.

Symbolic Nature of Early Christian Art.

The "domestic" nature of Christian art is shown by a quotation from the Early Church Father, Clement of Alexandria (c. 150 - c. 215). He is instructing Christians as to what sort of personal seals they should use. The seal was a way of signing a document and often showed a pagan god or symbol. Clement wrote to Christians:

> Now our seals ought to be a dove or a fish or a ship running before the breeze or a tuneful harp or a ship's anchor. And if there should happen to a fisherman, he will call to mind the apostle and the children drawn up from the water. We must not engrave our ring with the faces of idols, nor is a sword or bow appropriate to those who seek after peace nor wine cups to those who live a life of sobriety.[27]

The use of symbols is a very complex thing. They are not just simply short hand ways of giving information. In some ways, symbols manage to link different objects and ideas and give a deeper insight into their relationship. All human societies use symbols in one form or another. Jesus made great use of symbols and symbolic language to communicate his message and to describe himself. At one level, we have the parables which contain deep theological truths in the form

---

[27] *Paedagogos* 3. 59.2.

of a short simile or a much longer narrative. When describing himself Jesus used many symbols, "I am the vine", "I am the Good Shepherd", "I am the Door." The Holy Spirit is seen in the form of a dove. In all these ways, Jesus shows that the significance of his person and his message goes beyond the limits of his own time, and is an essential element in human life, something which everyone needs and can have access to. Symbols allowed the Early Church to paint images of invisible realities, like the soul, grace and everlasting life. The use of symbols was not unique to Christians, as pagan art and decoration was already rich in their use. This gave the added advantage that Christian art could be displayed in semi-public places such as homes and burial grounds, but only the initiated would be able to recognise the Christian significance of the common pagan-Christian symbols. Among the Early Christian symbols we find the ship. This can stand for hope in a future life, or a journey across the waters of death to the kingdom of God. The mast of the ship can stand for the Cross. The Cross was a common means of execution in the Roman Empire, and an image of a Cross would have scandalised a pagan. Christians therefore used symbols to stand for the Cross. Sometimes they used a ladder, which looks a little like a Cross, but also holds the idea that through the Cross we reach up to heaven. A tree could also stand for the Cross, as well as reminding Christians of the words of Psalm 1:3, which talks about the just person who is like a tree planted by streams of water that yield its fruit in its season. The palm frond was a pagan symbol of victory, and was often used by Christians to stand for the victory of Christ and the martyrs. One of the most famous Early Christian symbols is the fish. This symbol was chosen because the Greek word for fish is "ichthys," and the letters that make up the word can stand for "Jesus Christ Son of God (and) Saviour. As Clement pointed out, the fisherman could stand for an apostle, but a shepherd could also stand for the Good Shepherd. The figure of the shepherd, representing the joy of a simple country life, was also common in pagan art. The Early Church made even bolder use of pagan figures in a symbolic way by using the image of the Sun God to stand for Jesus, and well as the figure of the poet Orpheus who, like Jesus, descended into the land of the dead and rescued souls. By using these figures that were common in both Christian and pagan art, much that had Christian meaning could be used publicly without offending or antagonising the Roman state. As the Christians became more and more powerful and self-confident, this symbolic type of art almost disappeared.

The Catacombs

The catacombs of Rome play a very important part in the history of Christian art. It is in these burial tunnels that the earliest examples of recognisably Christian painting are found (c. 200 CE). The romantic idea that Early Christians conducted their entire religious lives in these cemeteries is exaggerated. It is clear that these extensive tunnels could not have been dug and used without the knowledge of the Roman civil authorities. In fact, in the earliest catacombs, there are examples of Christians and pagans being buried in close proximity. The Latin Christian Father St. Jerome has left us a description of what these underground cemeteries are like. He wrote:

> When I was young and being educated in Rome it was my custom every Sunday, along with other boys of my own age and tastes, to visit the tombs of the apostles and martyrs and enter the crypts excavated in the very bowels of the earth. The walls on both sides as you go in are full of dead bodies and the whole place is so murky that one seems almost to find the fulfilment of those words of the prophet, "Let them go down alone into Hell". Here and there a little light coming in from above is sufficient to give a momentary relief from the horror of darkness ...[28]

The word "catacomb" originally meant "by the hollow," and was a description of a particular district of Rome. The soil around Rome (and a few other cities in the Empire) made it ideal for digging these tunnels and shafts. In fact there are fifty-sixty distinct catacombs in Rome. It seems that catacombs began as family crypts, but gradually the larger community began to be buried in them as well. As the Church became more prosperous, catacombs reserved solely for Christians became common. The result of this "christianisation" of the catacombs was that the art work found in them is more clearly Christian in theme and less cryptic and symbolic. For example, the bishops and more wealthy members of the church constructed small chapels in the catacombs, and here funeral or commemorative meals were eaten. Often the walls of these small chapels were decorated with murals of the deceased soul enjoying a banquet in paradise. Also, as the numbers of martyrs grew, their graves became the object of devotion, and murals showing their life and death became common. In the final stages of catacomb art, patrons commissioned devotional images of Christ enthroned as Lord of All, and even the Virgin Mary enthroned. These images reflected the growing certainty of the Church that after the end of persecution and the advent of the edit of Milan (313 CE), the Church had emerged as conqueror of the pagan Empire.

From Catacomb to Basilica

As Christianity moved from a tolerated religion to being the official religion of the empire, it abandoned the catacombs and the small "house Churches" in favour of much larger buildings. At this point, painting (which was quick and cheap) gave way to the use of mosaic. The Church seemed to move with ease from the simple and symbolic art forms to a fully-fledged programme of religious decoration. The

---

[28] St Jerome *Commentarii in Ezecheielem*, PL, XXV,15.

bishop and poet St. Paulinus of Nola (353-431 CE) gives a good insight into the way this happened. St. Paulinus lived near the church built on the site of the tomb of St. Felix (c. 260 CE) The tomb of the saint attracted many pilgrims from the countryside, whose idea of celebrating the life of the saint was to eat, drink and be merry at his tomb. St. Paulinus tells us that the paintings of the life of St. Felix were there to instruct the uneducated country people and lift their minds from food to God. He wrote:

> This is why we thought it useful to enliven all the house of Felix with paintings on sacred themes, in the hope that they would excite the interest of the rustics by their attractive appearance for the sketches are painted in various colours. Over them are explanatory inscriptions, the written word revealing the theme outlined by the painter's hand. So when all the country folk point out and read over to each other the subjects painted they turn more slowly to thoughts of food, since the feast of fasting is so pleasant to the eye...[29]

The idea that pictures in the Church are the Bible of the illiterate was used as a common defence of Christian art. Nevertheless, the use of art in the service of the Church was not universally accepted, as we shall see later.

Legends of the first Icons

Two very important legends grew up around the images of Jesus and the Virgin Mary that show us how the Church sought to understand the relationship between theology and art. The first legend deals with the "Image not made by human hands" or the "Mandylion." This is an icon of the face of Christ which is shown reproduced on a piece of cloth. According to the legend, the King of Edessa, Abgar, asked Jesus to come to his city to cure him of a serious illness. Jesus declined, but sent an image of himself miraculously stamped on a linen cloth. This image was taken back to Edessa where it cured the king and was eventually placed over the city gate. During a period of persecution, the image was hidden, but was re-found in the sixth century, when it became an object of a cult that spread throughout the Christian world. Eventually, it was taken to Constantinople, but disappeared when the city was sacked by the Latin Crusaders in 1204. The idea of the "true image" (or Vera icona) is found in many forms in the devotional life of both the Eastern and Western Church: the true image of the Shroud of Turin; the fourth station of the Cross (Veronica wipes the face of Jesus); and the devotion to "the Holy Face". The historical origin of these images is impossible to trace much further than the sixth century, but all these devotions show the desire of the Church to see the face of Christ. As Hans Belting writes:

---

[29] Carmina 27.

God himself they (the Christians) now claimed, had in his
philanthropy provided a visible proof of his incarnation in the
form of the miraculous image, and also had thereby permitted
the making of images.[30]

The second legend deals with the icons of the Virgin Mary. Tradition states that St.
Luke painted three icons of the Virgin Mary after Pentecost: two with the Christ
child and a third by herself. The first icon is called "Hodighitria" (She who points
the way. The proper icon of our lady of *Perpetual Help* is of this first type. This is
an austere icon and both the Christ Child and the Virgin look directly at the viewer.
The second icon is called Eleousa (Our Lady of Tenderness). In this icon the
Mother and Child gently caress each other. The icon of the Virgin alone shows her
at prayer. Almost all Byzantine icons of the Virgin are variations on these themes.
Belief in an icon painted by St Luke, again goes back to the sixth century, but it is
impossible to verify the truth of the legend from an historical point of view. What
we do know is that the Early Church tended to attribute to the apostles any tradition
that was considered to be very old and dating back longer that the living memory
of the community. However, before dismissing the "apostolic origins" of Early
Christian traditions, we must remember that the accurate passing on of knowledge
from one generation to another was of vital importance in the past.

Thus, it seems that despite theoretical (and even Biblical) opposition to images,
the Early Church used art to express her faith. The real test of the validity of this
use came only in the eighth century. During this period, especially in the East, the
whole history of Christian art became a battle-ground for theological controversy.
Every Scriptural quotation and quotation from the Fathers was subjected to debate.
Much of the art of the fifth to the seventh century was destroyed by those who were
against images. For this reason it is very difficult for us to form an objective and
complete view of the origins of Christian art.

---

[30]   Hans Belting, *Likeness and Presence: A History of the Image Before the Era of Art*, trans. Edmund Jephcott
       (Chicago: University of Chicago Press, 1997), 56.

CHAPTER FOUR

ICONOCLASM AND THE SEVENTH ECUMENICAL COUNCIL

The use of images in the Church had always met with some form of opposition, which ranged from mild disdain for the need of those weak in faith for the support of the visual and pleasing, to the violent denunciation of icons as idolatry and superstition. All of this historical material is very difficult to judge in context. Suddenly, in 726 CE, the Byzantine Emperor Leo III (717-775 CE) began a systematic destruction of religious images throughout his Empire. The reason for this sudden outbreak of iconoclasm (icon breaking) is still a puzzle for historians. It was met with stiff opposition, especially from monks, and the battle was to last over 100 years. Finally, the iconodules (those who wished to keep icons) won the day. At the end of this period, images, especially for the Eastern Church, would almost rival the sacrament of the Eucharist as a means of expressing God's presence in the Church. Although this dispute was basically theological, the political situation of the Byzantine Empire, and that of Western Europe in the eighth to ninth centuries, influenced the religious debate. In fact, the shape of our contemporary world began to emerge at this time and, in a way, it is a result of the victory of the pro-icon party over the icon destroyers.

Political Background

The European world of the eighth and ninth century was a world dominated by Christianity. Nevertheless, this Christian world had been built on the foundations of the later Roman Empire. The Empire covered all the then known world; that is, from the English-Scottish border in the West to the Euphrates river in the East. All this area was subject to the Roman Emperor and controlled by the Roman army. By the fourth century CE, it was impossible to centrally administer the Empire from the city of Rome, so the Empire was eventually split in two Western and Eastern administrations. The capital of the Eastern Empire was the city of New Rome, which came to be known by the name of its founder, the Emperor Constantine (Constantinople). Even as the Western half of the Empire fell into political chaos due to a series of invasions by tribal peoples from the North and central Europe, the Eastern Empire continued to flourish as a Christian empire ruled by the "Roman" Emperor. Many of the historical forces at work in Western Europe did not touch the Eastern or Byzantine Empire. In the West, the centralised state collapsed and various tribal leaders sought to impose their rule on limited areas. This localised rule was in constant conflict with the knowledge that before the arrival of the so-called "barbarians," Western Europe had been one political unity. No leader could take the place of the Emperor. In fact, many in the West still looked to the Eastern Emperor as the real ruler of both halves of the empire. The relationship between the emerging nations of Western Europe and the Church also had no parallel in the Eastern Empire. The Pope in Rome found now himself confronted by a political and cultural vacuum that only the Church could fill. Culture and intellectual life became almost the monopoly of monks and priests, while the Pope became a sort of umpire between the warring nations of Europe and at other times the representative of the Eastern Emperor. In the West, the relationship between the Church and the emerging states was turbulent, a struggle by the Church to maintain her independence in the face of the desire of civil leaders to dominate all aspects of life. In the East, the relationship between the State and the Church was quite different. The Emperor was seen as the protector of the Church and the head of a Christian people. This relationship was called "symphonia" (harmony). To Western eyes, this relationship seemed to be one of subjection of the Church to the State. During the Iconoclast conflict, both East and West had their views of this relationship confirmed. From the Western point of view the Emperor had no right to meddle in the affairs of the Church. The question of the role of images in the Church was a question for the Pope and the bishops to decide. From the Eastern point of view, the final victory over Iconoclasm was gained by the two women rulers, the Empress Irene (752-803 CE) and the Empress Theodora (842-867 CE), thereby demonstrating the vital role that the ruler has in protecting the Church from danger, but rather forgetful that it was the Emperor who had cause and perpetuated the controversy. The whole experience of Iconoclasm was the cause of deep mistrust between the Papacy and the Byzantine Empire. The Popes in Rome gradually turned to the powerful rulers of the Carolingian dynasty (which covered parts of Modern France and Germany) for protection from the bullying of the lesser barbarian tribal leaders. In fact, the Carolingian kings began to be called Emperors and regard themselves as equals to the Emperor in Byzantium.

By the end of the debate on images, many differences were to become evident between the Eastern and the Western Church. These differences led to misunderstandings that eventually caused a deepening division between East and West.

Outline of Events.

The battle over the place of icons in the Eastern Church is divided into two periods. The first period lasts from the first systematic destruction of religious images in about 726 CE, until the Second Council of Nicea in 787 CE. The second period lasts from the rejection of Nicea II by the Emperor Leo V in 815 CE to the final victory of the pro-icon party in 843 CE.

First period: 726-787 CE

There seems to be no single clear reason for the rejection of images by some of the eighth and ninth century Emperors of Byzantium. Some theories have been proposed that Islam and Judaism (both of which totally reject religious art) influenced the Emperors in their rejection of icons. The sudden rise of Islam in the seventh century came as a complete shock to the Byzantine Empire. This new and hitherto unknown enemy swept all before it. Ancient and important Christian centres such as Jerusalem, Antioch and Alexandria disappeared under the sea of Islam. It is difficult for us to appreciate how closely the Christians of the Eastern Empire identified religion and politics. The Byzantines were a very religious people, and they could only see the hand of God in this sudden destruction of a great part of their empire. In order to win back God's favour, the Emperors, beginning with Leo III (717-740 CE), began to destroy all religious images that he considered to be idols. Perhaps he was led to this action by the fact that Islam rejected images and seemed to enjoy God's favour. It may seem strange that a political crisis (the Islamic invasion) called forth a religious response. It also seems strange to us that the civil authorities should try and impose their own religious views on their fellow citizens. To most Byzantines (both those that supported the Emperor's views and those who opposed them), such a mixing of religion and politics seemed to be the will of God. As God's anointed and protector of Christians, the Emperor enjoyed great power in the Church. Leo III replaced the Patriarch of Constantinople, Germanus (715-730 CE), because he did not support the destruction of icons. Nevertheless, the emperor was not alone in his opinions, because many members of the educated class (among them bishops) agreed that the reverence shown by simple faithful to religious images was really a form of idolatry. To add to the popularity of Leo's new-found hatred of images was the fact that he began to have more success in war against the Arabs. This confirmed in the minds of many (especially the army) that God was pleased with Leo's theology.

It soon became known in the West that the Byzantine Emperor had deposed his Patriarch and was undertaking a systematic destruction of religious images. Pope Gregory III (731-741 CE) at once appealed to the Emperor to abandon this offensive behaviour and to return to the traditional faith of the Church. This appeal was completely ignored and to punish the Pope, the Emperor confiscated land owned by the Pope in the South of Italy and transferred Sicily and parts of Northern Greece from the religious authority of the Pope to that of his own Patriarch. The Pope found himself in a very difficult position. He depended on the Emperor to defend him from the barbarian Lombards that were claiming more and more of Italy for themselves, but at the same time the destruction of images was clearly against Christian tradition.

Leo was succeeded by his son Constantine V (740-775 CE). Constantine was a soldier by nature who spent most of his reign engaged in wars against the Arabs and also the Bulgarians who threatened the Empire from the north. He was a more convinced iconoclast than his father and was determined to stamp out all religious images. Opposition grew to this policy, especially from the monks. Constantine set about to break all opposition and many monks died or were imprisoned. In order to enshrine his anti-icon teaching, Constantine called a Council (Council of Hieria) in 754 CE. It believed that Satan "could not endure the sight of this adornment", and gradually brought back idolatry under the appearance of Christianity. As then Christ armed his apostles against the ancient idolatry with the power of the Holy Spirit, and sent them out into all the world, so has he awakened against the new idolatry his servants our faithful Emperors and endowed them with the same wisdom of the Holy Spirit.[31]

This is more or less the logical outcome of a simplistic reading of the Old Testament prohibition on images. However, the Christian iconoclasts had to produce a theological reason for the destruction of images. This reason may not seem as clear cut to us at first sight. Nevertheless, it is perhaps more important in the history of the development of a Christian theology of art. The acts of the iconoclast Council read:

> [The painter] makes an image and calls it Christ. The name
> Christ signifies God and man. Consequently it is an image of
> God and man, and consequently he has in his foolish mind, in
> his representation of the created flesh, depicted the Godhead
> which cannot be represented, and thus mingled what should not
> be mingled. Thus he is guilty of double blasphemy - the one in
> making an image of the Godhead, and the other by mingling the
> Godhead and manhood.[32]

What the iconoclasts attempted to say was that it was impossible to depict the real nature of Jesus, who is true God and true man. All the artist could do was to make a painting of a man, and any veneration shown to this painting was idolatry, worshiping something that was not God.

The teachings of the iconoclast council were not accepted by the Western Church, and the gulf between East and West grew. At the same time the situation of the Papacy was growing worse because of the Lombard threat. Pope Stephen III (752-757 CE), in his short reign, broke all links with the Byzantine Emperor and turned for protection to the king of Franks. This was the beginning of the deepening involvement of the papacy in the political life of Western Europe. Nevertheless, the popularity of the iconoclast Emperor grew because of his military success. On the death of Constantine V, his son Leo IV (775-780 CE) continued his father's iconoclast policy, but on his death his wife Irene (752–803 CE) became co-ruler with her son Constantine VI, who was then only ten years old. Irene was a fervent defender of icons and set about to undo all that the previous Emperor had done. In 787 CE, she finally managed to call together a council of bishops

[31]   H.R.Percival, trans., *The Seven Ecumenical Councils of the Undivided Church* , vol 14 of *Nicene and Post-Nicene Fathers*, 2nd Series, ed. Philip Schaff and Henry Wace (Grand Rapids MI: W.B.Eerdmans, 1955), 543.

[32]   *The Seven Ecumenical Councils of the Undivided Church*, 543.

with representatives from the Pope of Rome and the Patriarchs of the other major Christian centres. This council, which was held in Nicea, close to Constantinople, is numbered as the Seventh Ecumenical (universal) Council. The council made a distinction between worship which we give to God alone, and reverence that we give to the Cross and to images of Jesus and the Saints. In the acts of the Council we read that it is good to be surrounded by images of Jesus and the Saints for the following reasons:

> The more often that they [Jesus and the Saints] are seen in artistic representations, the more often are we uplifted by the memory of their prototypes, and brought to a longing for them; and these images should be given reverence, but not the worship of faith which is due to the divine nature alone; but to these images, just as to a representation of the precious and life giving Cross and to the Book of the Gospels and to other holy objects, incense and lights may to offered according to ancient pious custom. For the honour which is paid to the image passes on to that which the image represents, and the one who reveres the image reveres in it the person represented.[33]

Second Period: 815-843 CE

After the Council of Nicea II, the Byzantine Empire did not enjoy a period of peace. The wars with the Arabs and the northern Bulgarians continued. The Empress Irene was unwilling to share power with her son, so she had him blinded, and she herself was forced from power by a "palace revolution" in 802. The man who replaced her, Nicephorus I, was killed in a battle with the Bulgarians in 811 CE, and the lack of military success following the Council of Nicea led many to consider that the return of the icons was a mistake. Thereafter, the rulers of the Empire from 811-842 returned to the iconoclast theology of the pre-Council period. The last iconoclast ruler was Theophilus, who died in 842 CE. At his death, the same situation that preceded the Second Council of Nicea (787 CE) repeated itself. Theophilus had left a young son (Michael III) whose mother, Theodora, acted as regent. Just as before, the Empress belonged to the pro-icon faction, and she quickly called a synod to restore the use of images in public worship. The restoration of icons is celebrated every year in the Byzantine Church on the first Sunday of Lent. Although the long dispute had left the Byzantine Empire divided, these divisions no longer showed themselves as quarrels over icons.

Leo Donald Davis, in his book *The First Seven Ecumenical Councils (325-787 CE): Their History and Theology* sums up the importance of the image controversy as follows:

---

[33] *The Seven Ecumenical Councils of the Undivided Church*, 550.

Politically, it was a factor in the alienation of the West from the Eastern Empire at a critical moment. The popes in Rome were under pressure from the encroaching Lombards and feared that the conquest of Rome by these Germans would reduce them to mere court chaplains. Opposed as they were to iconoclasm, the popes could expect no help from the emperor at Constantinople, busily stripping the icons from the churches. Thus Pope Zachary gave Pepin of the Franks moral support in his effort to win the crown from the do-nothing Merovingian kings in return for military help against the Lombards. Pope Stephen would go further to accept temporal control of the old Byzantine provinces in central Italy, thus founding the Papal States claimed by the popes until the Lateran Treaty with Mussolini in 1929. In 800 Pope Leo III crowned Charlemagne emperor of the West, creating a new defender of papal authority, who turned out to be as ready to dictate theology to the Church as his eastern counterparts.

Artistically, iconoclasm arrested progress and destroyed countless ancient treasures. Had iconoclasm become the official teaching of the Church the western world would never have witnessed the glorious achievements of its figured sacred art. It would have been immeasurably poorer artistically. After the iconoclast interlude, Byzantine art rose to new heights and continued to exert strong influence on the West, inheritors of the geometric interlace and stylised animals of Germanic art.[34]

Although these considerations seem to lead us a long way from purely artistic considerations, they show clearly that the battle for the survival of Christian art had far reaching implications which are still experienced today.

---

[34] Leo Davis, *The First Seven Ecumenical Councils (325-787): Their History and Theology* (Wilmington, Delaware: Michael Glazier, 1987), 318-319.

CHAPTER FIVE

THEOLOGY OF THE ICON DEFENDERS (ICONOPHILES)

D uring the conflict of the iconoclastic period there were many important members of the hierarchy of the Church, such as Patriarch Germanus of Constantinople (715-729 CE) and Pope Gregory II of Rome (714-731 CE), who defended the use of holy images in the Eastern Church. The defenders, or iconophiles, were fortunate in possessing several dynamic theologians who were able to refute the iconoclastic positions by showing that the veneration of icons was not idolatry. John Damascene (c. 652 - c. 750 CE), a monk and inspired theologian, provided the best defence of the use of icons in the life of the church through three Apologetic Discourses to those who Defame the Holy Icons.[35] His work contributed towards the final iconophile victory at the Seventh Ecumenical Council of Nicea (787 CE), and influenced other iconophiles who lived during the second period of iconoclasm (815-845 CE), such as St. Theodore of Studios (759-826 CE). [36]

St. John Damascene (c. 652-c. 750 CE)

St. John Damascene wrote his *Discourses on Defense of Divine Images* from his monastery at St. Saba, near Jerusalem, where he was relatively safe from the power and rule of the iconoclastic Emperor.[37] At the beginning of the first discourse, St. John draws attention to the far-reaching implications of iconoclasm on the church. He writes:

> I see the Church which God founded on the Apostles and Prophets, its corner-stone being Christ His Son, tossed on an angry sea, beaten by rushing waves, shaken and troubled by the assaults of the evil spirits. I see rents in the seamless robe of Christ, which impious men have sought to part asunder, and His body cut into pieces, that is, the word of God and the ancient tradition of the Church.[38]

Like a storm at sea, iconoclasm attacked the very foundation of the Church. Iconoclasm shook and troubled the Church by its reliance on the mistaken assumption that the Church can fall and had actually fallen into idolatry, and needed to be restored. John Damascene argues that iconoclasm's call for the

---

[35] G.Dragas, "St John Damascene's Teaching about Holy Icons," in *Icons: Windows on Eternity*, ed. G. Limouris (Geneva: WCC Publications, 1990), 53.

[36] K.Parry, "John of Damascus," in *The Blackwell Dictionary of Eastern Christianity* . ed. Ken Parry et al. (Oxford, UK: Blackwell Publishers, 2000), 270-271.

[37] Jim Forest, *Praying with Icons* (Maryknoll, NY: Orbis Books, 2002), 8. Damascene was relatively safe because the Monastery was in an area under Islamic rule.

[38] John Damascene, *Apologia of St John Damascene Against Those Who Decry Holy Images* 2004 http://www. balamand.edu.lb/theology/WritingsSJD.htm [accessed 8 August 2010], *First Treatise*, 1.

Church's restoration is wrong in self because the Church is essentially inerrant and is measured by its own ancient Tradition. He understands that the danger of iconoclasm to the unity of the Church – by its defiance of the Church's established Tradition – is a problem that concerns the truth, and especially the truth of what we know about God. Consequently, John Damascene directs his work towards the defence of the truth.[39] It is imperative that the truth about "the *personal* character of God," [40] that is, "the invisible God who became visible by assuming visible form," be defended.[41]

The Truth about God.

John Damascene reminds us that we receive the truth about God by revelation. In the Old Testament we learn that God is "one God, the source of all things, without beginning, uncreated, immortal, everlasting, incomprehensible, bodiless, invisible, uncircumscribed, without form."[42] Consequently, in Old Testament times, "God the incorporeal and uncircumscribed was never depicted."[43] In the New Testament this invisible, uncircumscribed God is revealed to us in the mystery of the Incarnation; that is, in the person of Jesus Christ, the Word made flesh.[44] In and through this mystery we learn that God is Father, Son and Holy Spirit and that Jesus is himself God, the invisible God of Israel, who has broken into human history and united himself to our visible human nature.[45] As a result, Christians must venerate and worship God in and through the humanity of Christ. It is due to this truth about God that John Damascene is able to say:

> I venture to draw an image of the invisible God, not as invisible,
> but as having become visible for our sakes through flesh and
> blood. I do not draw an image of the immortal Godhead. I paint
> the visible flesh of God, for it is impossible to represent a spirit,
> how much more God who gives breath to the spirit.[46]

Old Testament Prohibition of Images (Icons)

John Damascene begins the development of his theological defence of icons by refuting the argument against the drawing of images based on the Old Testament prohibition in Deuteronomy (6:13) and Exodus (20:4). He argues that a proper study of the Scriptures persuades us that the argument put forward by the iconoclasts is

---

[39] Dragas, "St John Damascene's Teaching about Holy Icons", 54.
[40] Daniel Sahas, *Icon and Logos: Sources in Eighth-Century Iconoclasm* (Toronto: University of Toronto Press, 1986), 6.
[41] Dragas, "St John Damascene's Teaching about Holy Icons", 54.
[42] Damascene, *Apologia – First Treatise*, 1.
[43] Damascene, *Apologia – First Treatise*, 4.
[44] Dragas, "St John Damascene's Teaching about Holy Icons", 54
[45] Lawrence.Cross, *Eastern Christianity. The Byzantine Tradition*, rev. ed. (Virginia, USA: Eastern Christian Publications, 1991), 33.
[46] Damascene, *Apologia – First Treatise*, 2; See also, Dragas, "St John Damascene's Teaching about Holy Icons", 54

based on a misunderstanding of the above texts. Other texts from Deuteronomy (e.g. 4:12, 15-17, 19; 5:7-9; 12:3) and Exodus (e.g. 34:17) reveal that the real aim of the Old Testament prohibition of images of God is that only the Creator, and not any created thing, should be worshipped, and that the veneration of worship should be rendered to God alone. Consequently, the Hebrews, who were prone to worshipping idols as gods (Ex 32:1ff), were prohibited from making images on account of idolatry and on account of the impossibility of making an image of the "immeasurable, uncircumscribed, invisible God."[47]

In view of the true intention of the texts, argues John Damascene, it is important to make the distinction between the Old Testament prohibition to the Hebrews against idolatry and God's revelation in the person of Jesus Christ, through which it is possible to distinguish between what can and cannot be depicted. It is impossible for those of the Old Testament to depict the incorporeal and invisible God (Ex 33:20), whereas those of the New Testament are able to depict the corporeal form of the invisible God. The thought of John Damascene is summed up as follows:

> When the Invisible One becomes visible to flesh, you may then draw a likeness of His form. When He who is a pure spirit, without form or limit, immeasurable in the boundlessness of His own nature, existing as God, takes upon Himself the form of a servant in substance and in stature, and a body of flesh, then you may draw His likeness, and show it to anyone willing to contemplate it. Depict His ineffable condescension, His virginal birth, His baptism in the Jordan, His transfiguration on Thabor, His all-powerful sufferings, His death and miracles, the proofs of His Godhead, the deeds which He worked in the flesh through divine power, His saving Cross, His Sepulchre, and resurrection, and ascent into heaven. Give to it all the endurance of engraving and color. Have no fear or anxiety; worship is not all of the same kind.[48]

Veneration and Icons

John Damascene points out that both the drawing and veneration of icons present no problem as Scripture witnesses to various kinds of worship, such as Abraham's veneration of the impious sons of Emmor (Gen 23:7; cf Acts 7:16) and Jacob's veneration of his brother Esau (Gen 33:3). He asserts that these venerations did not amount to an offering of worship. They were venerations on account of honour, which are noticeably different from the veneration of worship that is offered to God alone.[49] It is at this point that John Damascene analyses the exact meaning of

---

[47]   Damascene, *Apologia - First Treatise*, 2; See also, Dragas, "St John Damascene's Teaching about Holy Icons", 54-55.

[48]   Damascene, *Apologia – First Treatise*, 3; See also, Dragas, "St John Damascene's Teaching about Holy Icons", 55.

[49]   Dragas, "St John Damascene's Teaching about Holy Icons", 55.

icons and veneration. He says, "an image is a likeness of the original with a certain difference, for it is not an exact reproduction of the original."[50] John Damascene provides examples of a variety of types of icons to demonstrate that the logic and purpose of each type of icon governs the veneration that is given to them. He explains that there are three different degrees of veneration, namely: veneration which as worship, is offered to God alone; veneration which is offered to God's saints and servants by association, because of God who alone is naturally venerable; and veneration that is offered by one human being to another. He concludes that one either does away with veneration all together, or one accepts these kinds of veneration.[51]

Old Testament Commands and Icons

John Damascene refutes the argument against the making of icons, an argument based on the Mosaic Law and does so on the very basis of the Old Testament itself. He argues that if God is the only one Lawgiver, and that the Law is not to be regarded as contradictory, then it is important to state the correct meaning of both the prohibition of images and the commands related to the making of icons. He explains that since it is not possible for God to be imaged, lest that image becomes an object of worship, God commanded, for example, the making of the two Cherubim on either side of the Mercy-seat to represent the angelic Cherubim who stand before God's throne (Ex 25:18) and who overshadow the Mercy-seat, itself an icon of the divine mysteries. These divine mysteries, made out of matter, were icons of heavenly realities intended by God to be used by the priests in the worship of the one true God (Heb 8:5). God forbade the making of idols and the worship of idols as gods, but God did not forbid the making of icons used in the worship of the one true God. St. John Damascene concludes by saying that it makes no sense, therefore, to maintain that the Law prohibits the making of icons altogether.[52]

The Incarnation, Icons of God and Matter

St. John explains that the Church's tradition for the making and veneration of icons of God comes from the Incarnation. He says:

> Of old, God the incorporeal and uncircumscribed was never
> depicted. Now, however, when God is seen clothed in flesh,
> and conversing with men (Bar. 3:37), I make an image of the
> God whom I see. I do not worship matter, I worship the God of

---

[50] Damascene, *Apologia – First Treatise*, 3; See also, Dragas, "St John Damascene's Teaching about Holy Icons", 56.

[51] Damascene, *Apologia – First Treatise*, 4; See also, Dragas, "St John Damascene's Teaching about Holy Icons", 56-57.

[52] Damascene, *Apologia – First Treatise*, 4; See also, Dragas, "St John Damascene's Teaching about Holy Icons", 57. G.Turpa, *Icons: Aids in Spiritual Struggle* http://www.stuladimis.ca/library/icons-spiritual-struggle.htm [accessed 7 September 2004].

matter, who became matter for my sake, and deigned to inhabit matter, who worked out my salvation through matter. I will not cease from honouring that matter which works my salvation.[53]

Christians clearly believe that matter is good and suitable for the worship of God (see Gen 2:31; Ex 35:4-10). Christians honour matter, says John Damascene, "not as God, but as a channel of divine strength". He goes on to say:

> Was not the thrice blessed wood of the Cross matter? and the sacred and holy mountain of Calvary? Was not the holy sepulchre matter, the life-giving stone the source of our resurrection? Was not the book of the Gospels matter, and the holy table which gives us the bread of life? Are not gold and silver matter, of which crosses, and holy pictures, and chalices are made? And above all, is not the Lord's Body and Blood composed of matter? Either reject the honor and worship of all these things, or conform to the ecclesiastical tradition, sanctifying the worship of images in the name of God and of God's friends, and so obeying the grace of the Divine Spirit.[54]

Icons of the Saints

Those who object to the icons of the saints, according to John Damascene, reject the honour and glorification of the saints. Since Scripture teaches us that God will glorify those who glorify Him (1 Sam 2:30), and that we will be like God when we see God as God really is (1 Jn 3:2) then the saints, who are united with God, become glorified and deified. Thus, whatever belongs to the nature of the saints, whether spiritual or material, is filled with the sanctifying energy of God's Spirit. As heirs of God and co-heirs of Christ (Rom 8:17), the saints are partakers of God's glory and kingdom in heaven and on earth. Hence, they should not be deprived of the honour given to them by the Church. John Damascene concludes by saying:

> I worship the image of Christ as the Incarnate God; that of Our Lady ... the Mother of us all, as the Mother of God's Son; that of the saints as the friends of God. They have withstood sin unto blood, and followed Christ in shedding their blood for Him, who shed His blood for them. I put on record the excellencies and the sufferings of those who have walked in His footsteps, that I may sanctify myself, and be fired with the zeal of imitation. St Basil says, 'Honouring the image leads to the prototype.'[55]

---

[53] Damascene, *Apologia – First Treatise,* 4; See also, Dragas, "St John Damascene's Teaching about Holy Icons", 57.
[54] Damascene, *Apologia – Second Treatise,* 5; See also, Dragas, "St John Damascene's Teaching about Holy Icons", 63-64.
[55] Damascene, *Apologia – First Treatise,* 6; See also, Dragas, "St John Damascene's Teaching about Holy Icons", 60.

The veneration of honour extended to an icon passes on to the prototype, that is, to the person who is represented on the icon, because the person who venerates an icon venerates the person represented on the icon .[56] The icon is not identical to the prototype, but is connected to the prototype because it represents the person and carries the person's name.[57]

Theodore of Studios (759-826 CE)

Like John Damascene, St. Theodore of Studios believed that iconoclasm attacked the reality of the Incarnation and the possibility of God's revelation to us through matter. Thus, Theodore sought both to restore the emphasis on the reality of Christ's humanity and to show how this was at one with the making and veneration of icons. In basing his iconology on the distinction between circumscribed and uncircumscribed, and on the principle that anything circumscribed can be painted and anything uncircumbscribed cannot, Theodore argued that when the Word became flesh, Christ – like any other human individual – can be depicted in a painted image. In Theodore's writings *On the Holy Icons*, we read:

> There is a mixture of the immiscible, a compound of the uncombinable; that is of the uncircumscribable with the circumscribed, of the boundless with the bounded, of the limitless with the limited, of the formless with the well formed (which is indeed paradoxical). For this reason Christ is depicted in images, and the invisible seen. He who is in His own divinity is uncircumscribable accepts the circumscription natural to His body.[58]

In other words, the icon of Christ does not represent Christ's human nature or divine nature, but Christ's *person* which "inconceivably unites in itself these two natures without confusion and without division."[59] It testifies to the unity of the humanity and divinity of Christ, and to the distinction between what is created and uncreated as the image is a representation of the one uncircumscribed Word who, taking flesh, became circumscribed.[60] The person of Christ is represented in the icon, and in his person Christ's divine and human natures shine through.[61]

---

[56] "The Veneration of Icons in the Tradition of the Byzantine Rite" http://www.byzantines.net/moreinfo/ veneratelcons.htm, [accessed 12 August 2004], 4. See also, J.Brentnall, "The Language of Orthodox Icons: A Resource For Teachers Of Religious Education " http://www.farmington.ac.uk/documents/old_docs/Brentnall.htm [accessed 12 August 2004], 5.

[57] Leonide Ouspensky, *Theology of the Icon* (Crestwood, NY: St Vladimir's Seminary Press, 1978), 153.

[58] Cited in Stephen Bigham, *The Image of God the Father in Orthodox Theology and Iconography and Other Studies* (Torrance CA: Oakwood Publications, 1995), 36.

[59] Ouspensky, *Theology*, 152

[60] C. Scouteris, "Never as Gods : Icons and their Veneration " http://www.orthodoxresearchinstitute.org/articles/ liturgics/scouteris_icons.htm [accessed 7 September 2004].

[61] Brentnall, "The Language of Orthodox Icons", 3.

Theodore affirms that the incarnate Christ both can and must be portrayed in an image in order to assert that God had entered into the world of matter, in the Word made flesh, and has restored God's own image in humanity. Since God had been revealed in the flesh, Theodore argues that both hearing and seeing are necessary for a full absorption of what has been revealed in Christ. St. Theodore says, Christ ...

> nowhere told anyone to write down the "concise word"; yet his image was drawn in writing by the apostles and has been preserved up to the present. Whatever is marked there with paper and ink, the same is marked on the icon with various pigments or some other material. For the great Basil says: 'Whatever the words of the narrative offer, the picture silently shows by imitation.' [62]

Sts. John and Theodore, in their theological defense of the veneration of icons, remained faithful to the tradition of the Church, which from its earliest beginnings has treated icons as "an expression of the theological experience and faith of the Church, and a statement of it."[63] In arguing that Christ, his Mother Mary and the saints could be venerated in a material image, they were aware that the rejection of the divine images undermined the place of matter in the salvation of the world.[64] In denying the human image of God, iconoclasm refused to accept the consequences of the incarnation, that is, the "sanctification of matter in general and the deification of man in particular."[65] The iconophiles were defending the meaning of the Church's very existence, as iconoclasm attacked the whole economy of salvation, that is, the sanctification of the visible, material world.[66] The victory of Orthodoxy over the iconoclasts is best summed up in the Kontakion for the First Sunday of the Great Lent. It reads:

> No one could describe the Word of the Father, but when He took flesh from you, O Theotokos, He accepted to be described, and restored the fallen image to its former state by uniting it to divine beauty. We confess and proclaim our salvation in word and images.[67]

---

[62] Cited in J.Baggley, *Doors of Perception: Icons and their Spiritual Significance* (London: Mowbray, 1987), 23-24.
[63] Sahas, *Icons and Logos*, 5.
[64] D.Turner, "Iconoclasm," in *The Blackwell Dictionary of Eastern Christianity*, ed. Ken Parry et al. (Oxford: Blackwell, 2000), 239-242.
[65] Ouspensky, *Theology of the Icon*, 174.
[66] Ouspensky, *Theology of the Icon*, 175.
[67] G.Barrow, *The Iconoclastic Crisis* www.orthodoxresearchinstitute.org/articles/church_history/barrow_iconoclastic_crisis.htm [accessed 12 August 2004] , 3.

CHAPTER SIX

GENESIS OF THE ICON

W e do not know very much about the development or nature of Christian art in the first two centuries after the death of Jesus. During this period,the church was a relatively small, frequently persecuted group and, of necessity, any art it did develop was hidden or ephemeral. They also had little motivation to develop major, durable art works since they believed in the immanent return of Christ and waited expectantly for the immediate overthrow of the temporal order and the establishment the Kingdom of God.

Among the earliest examples of Christian Art still in existence are the early third century paintings on the walls of the catacombs in Rome. Since the catacombs were burial places, they were considered inviolate by Roman society, and the destruction of Christian art, which would have occurred elsewhere, did not occur here. It was in these hidden places that the despised and sometimes outlawed Christian religion could find its first public expression. The style of these early drawings resembles the naturalistic form of secular Roman wall painting. However, its quality was very much inferior. Indeed, it is almost cartoonish when compared to the sophisticated Roman art of the period. Roman artists boasted of being able to produce works of art so realistic that it would fool horses and birds. This is almost certainly exaggeration but the art of the catacombs could have no such pretensions.

One characteristic of this art was the extensive use of symbols, both pagan and Christian. Even when the subject matter consisted of realistically rendered biblical figures, such as Jonah, Daniel, or Susanna, they appear in scenes of miracles through divine intervention. It is the meaning of these figures which is being conveyed, not a portrayal of them as historical figures. When Christ is represented, it is often as an Apollo-like figure: youthful and with blond, curly hair.

The Christian symbols used were often mixed with pagan symbols, or had both a pagan and a Christian meaning. An example of a prominent Christian symbol is the fish, which in Greek (ICTHYS) is an anagram of 'Jesus Christ Saviour.' As well as this, it is a reference to Peter, the fisherman, and to the gospel story of the feeding of the five thousand. It is also an Egyptian symbol of resurrection. A ship can be a symbol of the ark, the church (particularly with the mast and yard arm arranged as a cross), or a reference to the apostles, the fishers of men. It is also a pagan symbol for the journey of the dead, particularly appropriate in a burial chamber. A dove can mean peace and immortality to a pagan and have the added meaning of the Holy Spirit to a Christian. A shepherd carrying a sheep on his shoulders would signify the personification of *philanthropia* (love of mankind) to the pagan Greeks and have the added meaning of Jesus as 'The Good Shepherd to the Christians' (see Figure 6.1).

Figure 6.1.
Image of Christ as the Good Shepherd from the Roman
Catacombs.

Even pagan legends, such as that of Orpheus, were reinterpreted in a Christian context. Note that the pagan and Christian meanings of these symbols are not contradictory; rather, the Christian reinterpretation adds both depth and reality to the pagan symbol. Eucharistic symbols such as grapes, bread and wine cups also feature significantly in this art. Peacocks, as a symbol of immortality, are borrowed directly from pagan art. It is worth noting that the cross does not feature as a prominent Christian symbol at this time.

There was a very significant difference in the intentions of pagan and Christian art, even when they were using essentially the same images. The pagan art was trying to realistically represent the physical world. Christian art was trying to represent a transcendent reality using symbols taken from the physical world. This abstraction of physical reality to represent a transcendent reality was to become a permanent, even a defining feature of Christian art. Two other features, which were to persist and later to become important, also feature at this early stage. These were the use of art as a teaching aid, as seen in the rendering of biblical themes, and its use in liturgy to define the character of a sacred place.

Following the official recognition of Christianity after the Edict of Toleration by the Emperor Constantine in 313 CE, the scope of Early Christian art was radically enlarged. The church now had to build and decorate large places of public worship, and from the very beginning it was clear that the church would insist that the art in these churches would not be mere decoration, but would have a spiritual purpose. Thus, in the fifth century, when the Prefect Olympiodorus suggested to St. Nilus of Sinai that a church which he had built should be decorated with animals and hunting scenes, St. Nilus replied:

> My answer to your letter is that it is infantile and dangerous to seduce the eye of the faithful with such things... Let the hand of the best painter cover both sides of the church with images from the Old and New Testaments, so that those who do not know the alphabet and cannot read Holy Scriptures will remember, while looking at the painted representations, the courageous deeds of those who served God without malice. Thus, they will be encouraged to emulate the ever-memorable virtues of these servants of God who preferred the heavens to the earth, and the invisible to the visible.[68]

Here we have an early expression of what was to become a recurring theme in church art in both the Eastern and Western churches: that art could be a teaching aid, a visual scripture for the illiterate. Ecclesial art had other purposes as well, and rapidly developed into an integrated system of imagery defining the church as a sacred place dedicated to worship.

> Elaborate mosaic narrative cycles covered the upper walls, triumphal arch, and apse of basilican churches. Some are preserved in Santa Maria Maggiore and Santa Pudenziana in Rome and Sant'Apollinare Nuovo in Ravenna. The use of gold backgrounds heightens the effect of otherworldliness and transcendence.....The entire church thus served as a tangible evocation of the celestial order; this conception was further enhanced by the stylized poses and gestures of the figures, their hieratic gaze, and the luminous shimmer of the gold backgrounds.[69]

Let us consider the following description by Jas Elsner of the Basilica of Saint Apollinare Nuovo in Ravenna (see Figure 6.2):

---

[68] Quoted in Ouspensky, *Theology of the Icon,* 104-105.
[69] *The Columbia Electronic Encyclopedia,* 6th ed. Columbia University Press, 2004.

Figure 6.2.
Mosaics from Saint Apollinare Nuovo, Ravenna.

The impact is one of longitudinal meditation. The viewer enters the church at the west and stands by the door below images of the world he or she knows, the world of the here and now. On the right if one faces the apse is the city of Ravenna and the palace of Theodoric, which in reality stood just outside the building and for which the basilica was originally the chapel. On the left is the port of Classe. As one proceeds up the nave, one leaves this space, the images of this world, and moves through a procession of martyrs – women and men who were once part of this world but whose self-immolation in the cause of the Faith has transported them to the Other World. Their very procession (as was their martyrdom) is an intercession for us, as we proceed past them towards the east........on the nave walls at the east are representations of Christ on the right and the Virgin on the left, each enthroned between angles. The mediating procession of martyrs has led us through St. Martin, the patron of this church, and the Magi, the scriptural witnesses of the Epiphany of the Incarnation, from the representations of this world to the images of the divine reality – the Other World. We have moved from the temporal to the eternal, from the specific (the here and now of Ravenna and its port) to the general (the forever here and now of the presence of God).[70]

As well as the church mosaics, Christian artists began to develop devotional panels,

---

[70] Jas Elsner, *Art and the Roman Viewer: The Transformation of Art from the Pagan World to Christianity* (Cambridge: Cambridge University Press, 1995), 223-232.

and it is here that the Icon, as it is commonly understood, came into being. A large collection of early devotional panels is preserved at St. Catherine's Monastery in Sinai. The Roman Empire was very cosmopolitan, with well established routes of trade and freely moving academics, artists and even clergy. Christian art began to absorb influences from all over the world. Apart from the obvious influence of Roman public art, there are three main influences that stand out in the development of the Christian Icon: Mummy portraits from Egypt, Hellenistic Art, and the art of Palmyra in Syria.

From Roman public art the Christian Icons, particularly in Church mosaics, took stylistically the formal, posed attitudes of the figures, and ontologically they embraced the idea that an image could make present what was depicted. Thus, an official image or statue of the Emperor stood in the place of the Emperor and to insult or to refuse to pay homage to such a statue was to insult or refuse to pay homage to the Emperor, and was dealt with in the same way. This idea passed into the theology of Christian Icons and was given added depth and impact through the Incarnation, the action of the Spirit, and the belief in sacramentality.

Important among the other influences were the mummy portraits of Christian Egypt. Early Christian Egyptians still followed the custom of having the dead mummified but they did away with the realistically-carved sarcophagi and death masks since they understood the Bible to prohibit carved and graven images. They had, however, no objection to paintings on a flat surface and considered these to be more spiritual (see Figure 6.3). More than 500 of these mummies have been excavated at the oasis of El Fayyum in the lake country situated 120 kilometres south of Cairo. All of these date from the between the first and fourth centuries CE, when Egypt was occupied by the Romans.

Figure 6.3.
Mummy Portrait from Ptolomaic Egypt.

Ironically, given the history that was to follow, the primitive, partial iconoclasm of these Egyptian Christians gave rise to an art form that was a major influence on later Christian Iconography. The portraits were using the medium of wax encaustic, and later egg tempera. Both are startlingly realistic. They show men and women with large eyes which seem to stare off into the distance, past the viewer. Although they have the accoutrements of this world, they are clearly already a part of the next world. Although the influence is disputed by some authors[71], the similarity with later iconography is marked.

The Greek, or Hellenistic, tradition was arguable the dominant artistic culture of the ancient world. Christian Icons gained a sense of grace and movement from this tradition, as well as concepts such as numerical symmetry and perspective. It was from this source that the distinctive use of parallel- and reverse-perspective developed. The geometrical balance and proportion of the Icon also derives from Hellenistic art (see Figure 6.4).

Figure 6.4.
Engraved Plate showing the Battle of David and Goliath from the Hellenistic Period (sixth century) showing the Greek sense of Proportion and Balance.

The realism of the icons comes from the art of Syria and Egypt. Thus, images of Christ as a blond curly haired youth, similar to representation of the Greek god Apollo, are replaced by a bearded, dark haired Aramaic - speaking Syrian. In images of Mary, the headdress and jewellery of a Roman matron is replaced by the long veil of a Syrian woman. The influence of Palmyra is felt in the confronting

---

[71] Ouspensky, *Theology of the Icon*, 107.

gaze of its subject. No longer do the portraits look past the viewer to a far distance. Influenced by Palmyra they engage the viewer, eye to eye

All of these artistic influences were combined with an intention not to reproduce the natural world, or to make an inferior copy of something, but to use the transformed image of the physical world to represent the transcendent reality of God. This was only possible because of the incarnation. Since, in Christ, the Divine Logos had taken physical form, the physical world had been transformed and it has become possible for the physical to represent the divine. Indeed, since the invisible and unknowable nature of God was present in the person of Jesus, the icon could, through the action of the Spirit, make present the reality it represented. The icon thus takes on a sacramental character. It is this understanding which is the distinctive mark of the Christian Icon. Ultimately, it is this which makes the icon different from all other art. The stylistic elements are only important in that they support and manifest this understanding.

This is not to say that the stylistic elements are not important. They provide the visual vocabulary through which the divine presence is communicated. These stylistic elements are discussed in other chapters. There are also traditional elements to iconography which enable the meaning and identity of the icon to be instantly recognised by those who know them. Thus, in the traditional representations of Saints Peter and Paul, Peter is shown as balding, with white curly hair and a beard, while Paul is represented as thinner, clean shaven, balder and with straight, dark hair. These are believed to be derived from the preserved folk memory of what Peter and Paul actually looked like. This interest in the true likeness of the subject is also present in the legend that the first portraits of Our Lady were painted by St. Luke from life, and that the traditional Marian icons thus preserve a true likeness of Mary.

This is even more true of the legend of the image of Christ not painted by human hands. In the East, this is the legend of King Abgar of Edessa, who asked Jesus, via a messenger, to come cure him. Jesus didn't come, but sent a miraculous image of his face on a linen cloth, which cured the king. This is similar to the story of Veronica in the Western church, who wiped the face of Jesus on the way to Calvary and was left with an image of his face imprinted on the cloth. The face seen in art derived from both of these legends is remarkably similar, somewhat long and bearded with a straight, prominent nose (see Figure 6.5). This is also the face on the Shroud of Turin. This "true image" of Christ is not only important in the iconography of the Eastern Church but has also dominated Western religious art.

Figure 6.5.
Nineteenth Century Russian Icon of the Mandylion,
the True Image of Christ.

The early development of the Christian Icon is well summarised in this statement of Ouspensky:

> To develop its language, the church used, as we have seen,
> forms, symbols and even myths of antiquity, i.e. pagan forms
> of expression. But it did not use these forms without purifying
> them and adapting them to its own goals. Christianity absorbs
> everything that can serve as a form of expression from the world
> around it. Thus the Fathers of the Church used all the apparatus
> of ancient philosophy for the benefit of theology. Similarly,
> Christian art inherits the best traditions of antiquity. It absorbs
> elements of Greek, Egyptian, Syrian, Roman and other arts,
> sacralizing this complex heritage, guiding it in expressing the
> fullness of its own meaning and transforming it in accordance
> with the requirements of Christian teaching.[72]

---

[72] Ouspensky, *Theology of the Icon*, 106.

CHAPTER SEVEN

REGIONAL DEVELOPMENT OF THE ICON

W hile it is true that the writing of an icon is a very restrictive art form and one where tradition allows little scope for the imagination of the individual artist, it is not true that icons are uniform across either time or space. As the theology of the icon developed, so did the icons themselves. As new saints entered into glory, so new icons were written to represent them. Icons written in one culture could be markedly different from icons written in another. This variation is to be expected as part of the glorious diversity of God's people.

> .....does not mean that the church suppresses the specific character of the cultural elements which it adopts. It excludes nothing which is a part of the nature created by God, not one human trait, not one indication of time and place, not one national or personal characteristic. It sanctifies all the diversity of the universe, revealing to it its true meaning, orienting it towards its true end: the building up of the Kingdom of God. Cultural diversity does not violate the unity of the Church, but offers it new forms of expression. Thus the catholicity of the Church is confirmed both in cultural wholeness and in the individual details. In the realm of art, just as in other areas, catholicity does not mean uniformity, but rather the expression of one truth in a variety of forms, characteristic of every people, of every epoch, of every man.[73]

There is a main line of tradition that has developed, however, in iconography. This is the tradition that began in Byzantium and was passed, via the Balkans, to ancient Rus. When people speak of Christian icons they normally mean images from this tradition. There is also a surprisingly complex relationship between the Icons of the Eastern Church and the devotional religious art of the Western Church. This interaction is strongest in the border kingdoms such as Cyprus and Romania. Other traditions such as the Coptic and Ethiopian tend to be of local importance only.

The Byzantine style

The beginnings of the Byzantine style can be traced at least to the rule of the Emperor Justinian, and can be seen in the mosaics of San Vitale in Ravenna and in mosaic fragments from Sancta Sophia, Constantinople (see Figure 7.1).

---

[73] Ouspensky, *Theology of the Icon*, 109.

Figure 7.1
Late Byzantine Icon of the Presentation in the Temple
(Fifteenth Century).

A large group of devotional images has also been preserved in the monastery of St. Catherine on Mt. Sinai. The style involves figures with a dignified bearing and with prominent eyes, looking past the viewer into eternity. After the iconoclast controversy, old techniques had to be re-evaluated. Mosaics were still used but encaustic (wax colour) techniques gave way to the use of egg tempera. Since the cult of icons played a leading part in both religious and secular life, an important aspect of Byzantine artistic activity was the painting of devotional panels (see Figure 7.1). Icon painting afforded little scope for individuality since the effectiveness of the religious image as a vehicle of divine presence was held to depend on its fidelity to an established prototype. The development of Byzantine painting may also be seen in manuscript illumination.[74]

Byzantine achievements in mosaics brought this art to an unprecedented and unsurpassed level of grandeur and expressive power. Mosaics were applied to nearly all of the available surfaces of Byzantine churches, but in an established hierarchical order. The centre of the dome was reserved for the representation of the Pantocrator or Jesus as the ruler of the universe, whereas other sacred personages occupied lower spaces in descending order of importance. The entire church thus served as a tangible evocation of the celestial order; this conception was further enhanced by the stylized poses and gestures of the figures, their hieratic gaze, and the luminous shimmer of the gold backgrounds (see Figure 7.2).

---

[74] *The Columbia Electronic Encyclopedia*, 6th ed. Columbia University Press, 2004.

Figure 7.2.
Mosaic of Christ the Life Giver with Mary and St. John the
Baptist. Sancta Sophia, Constantinople.

The Amorian dynasty (820-867) saw change in the Byzantine Empire. It became more Greek, and was reorganized in a way that brought church and state into harmony. This led to the establishment of elite icon workshops that used ivory, gold and enamel. There was also an increasing influence from both Sassanid Persian and Islamic Culture. The subsequent history of the empire saw a gradual decline in the quality of the icons and a shift in style away from dignified detachment. However, the late mosaics and frescos of the Chora Church in Constantinople (1313) (The Saviour in the fields) are among the finest examples of Byzantine art. Legend has it that some of these were still being painted even as the gates of the city were being bombarded. The sacred figures here are characterized by an energy, a sense of movement and a strange inner agitation which is absent from earlier works.

One region where the Byzantine style could survive and develop without the disruption of Islamic rule was Mt. Athos. This peninsula in northern Greece became a place of retreat for monks and hermits from the ninth century. In 1046, it was officially recognized, and even the Turks generally recognized its sovereignty as a monastic republic. The monks saw themselves as the caretakers of an unbroken tradition. Artists came to Mt. Athos from Greece, the Greek islands (including Cyprus and Crete), and even from the Venetian Empire from the eleventh century. In later times all Orthodox nations developed monastic communities at Athos and this has resulted in a richness and diversity of iconographic style (see Figure 7.3)

Figure 7.3
Frescos from a monastery on Mt. Athos

The Balkans

Thessalonika was the most significant Byzantine city after Constantinople. It was also of great significance because it was on the Balkan Peninsula, an area where both Rome and Byzantium interacted with Slavic tribes. It was here that orthodoxy was first passed to the Slavic peoples. A priest called Constantine (later named Cyril) invented the Old Slavic (Church Slavonic) alphabet to give the voiceless Slavic peoples a voice. Cyril and his brother Methodius were iconophiles during the iconoclast period, and they passed on the reverence for icons as well as the Byzantine style to the Christian Slavic tribes. This was very fruitful in that it led to the establishment of icon schools in the surrounding countries (Bulgaria and Serbia) and, ultimately, to the great icons schools of Russia.

In Bulgaria, the city of Ochrid achieved early prominence, as is evidenced by the eleventh century frescos in the church of Saint Sophia. Icons from the Ochrid School are marked by a certain elegance and restraint. The elaborate richness of the Byzantine style is subdued somewhat by exposure to native forms, and the result is the creation of a distinct national style. The city of Trnovo became a major centre of icon painting in the thirteenth and fourteenth centuries, and underwent a renaissance in the nineteenth century. Icons from Trnovo, which maintained a "pure", conservative style, helped to maintain a national religious identity, even during Turkish domination.

Serbian art was deeply influenced by political and religious turmoil. Its first independent leader, Grand Duke Stephan Nemanja, was a political foe of Byzantium, although he was greatly in awe of the Byzantine culture. This led to the adoption of Byzantine religious norms even though Serbia remained fiercely independent. Most Serbian icons are of a simple Slavic style, but many also show evidence of competition between the realism of early western Gothic elements and the formal idealism of late Byzantine or Greek elements. One other notable feature of Serbian iconography was the emphasis on tender, human images of Mary and her child. This was in response to the heretical threat of the Bogomils whose rejection of the incarnation precluded this kind of relationship between Mary and Jesus. There was also a great fondness for military saints such as St. George. The development of Serbian iconography effectively ended in 1389 when the kingdom was overrun by the Turks although, of course, there were still icons painted in rural villages.

While in no way denying the local importance of the icon art of the Balkans or even the significance of this art for the wider Christian community, it is probably true to say that the most significant outcome of the iconography of the Balkans was that it was the vehicle by which the tradition of Byzantium was passed on to Russia, and it was in Russia, free from the influence of the Islamic Turkish empire, that most of the later development in icon art occurred.

The Russian Tradition

Christianisation of Rus began in Kiev with the baptism of Grand Duke Vladimir in 988 CE, and in spite of attacks by the Mongols, rule by the Tartars and almost constant internal squabbles, a relatively continuous development of indigenous iconography was possible. According to Ouspensky and Lossky, it was in the centres of medieval Russia that the finest flowering of the icon tradition was achieved, centres such as Novgorod, Pskov snd Moscow.

> It is indeed given to Russia to produce that perfection of the pictorial language of the icon, which revealed with such great force the depth of meaning of the liturgic image, its spirituality. It can be said that if Byzantium was preeminent in giving the world theology expressed in words, theology expressed in images was given preeminently by Russia.[75]

Despite legends of very early icons, the beginnings of Russian iconography can be traced to the large scale church art – both mosaics and frescoes – in Kiev and Novgorod. Examples of this can still be seen in the Cathedral of Holy Wisdom in Kiev. Icons began to be imported from Greece, and indigenous schools then developed. Important here was the founding of the Monastery of the Caves – the

---

[75] Leonide Ouspensky and Vladimir Lossky, *The Meaning of Icons* (New York: St Vladimir's Seminary Press, 1989), 45.

beginning of monasticism in the lands of the Rus. Grand Duke Andrei left Kiev in the twelfth century to establish a new capital, Vladimir, and what would eventually become the Principality of Tver. It was here that the feast of the Protecting Veil of the Mother of God was first proclaimed and the icon for this feast was first written. Kiev was conquered and destroyed by the Mongols in 1240. It was some centuries before it would recover to again play an important part in the cultural life of Rus.

Novgorod is the second of the ancient centers of Russian Christianity. Saint Sophia, the Cathedral of Holy Wisdom, was first built in 989 CE. Located in the North West of Russia, close to the Finnish border lands, Novgorod was a fiercely independent and strong-willed city of merchants. The city state was only brought under the rule of Moscow by Ivan the Terrible in 1570. Novgorod sponsored the development of a large number of icon workshops (see Figure 7.4) whose icons were "...as lucid and unambiguous in composition and colouring as the business ledgers of the merchants who commissioned the works."[76] The faces often show the influence of the native Finnish population, and St. Nicholas is a favorite subject. Pskov is a smaller city within the territory of Novgorod, whose icons also have a marked somber atmosphere caused by the use of sulfuric arsenic in the paint.

Figure 7.4.
Icon of Saints John Climacos, George and Blaise from the
Novgorod School, Thirteenth Century.

---

[76] Konrad Onasch and Annemarie Schnieper, *Icons: The Fascination and the* Reality, trans. D. G. Conklin (New York: Riverside Book Company, Inc. 1997), 80.

Andrei Rublev is arguably the most famous of all iconographers. His icon of the Trinity (The Hospitality of Abraham) was written to affirm the orthodox understanding of the Trinity, and it has become famous, with copies spreading across both national and denominational borders (see Figure 7.5). Andrei Rublev lived between 1360 and 1427. He was a monk of the Andonikov Monastery in Moscow, which he only left to do commissioned work. All his icons are marked by a restrained and simple style which is seen as an expression of the asceticism of his life. This is particularly marked when compared to his famous contemporaries (or near contemporaries) Theophanes the Greek, an immigrant escaping from the Turkish assault on Byzantium who brought the skilled, elegant and expressive style of late Byzantium, and Dionysius, a layman who visualized the idea of Moscow as the third Rome with his complex biographical icons of major church figures. Dionysius is also well known for his Marian icons. Rublev, Theophanes and Dionysius represent the major strands in Russian Icon writing: the monastic schools, the Greek influence and the secular or state workshops respectively.

Figure 7.5
Icon of the Trinity by Andrei Rublev

The Moscow School arose from these diverse sources. It can really only be spoken of as a school because of the central political importance of Moscow. Beginning under the rule of the Tartars, and finally confirmed under the brutal rule of Ivan the Terrible in the middle to late sixteenth century, Moscow became the political and cultural capital of a developing Russian empire. The icons produced by this school represent a great elaboration from the simple prototypes. These icons will often contain large numbers of people, intricate detail and a strong narrative sense. They also show a strong political influence. This is perhaps best represented by the icon of the Church Triumphant, which shows various Russian military leaders, including Ivan the Terrible, marching in procession to heaven at the head of their armies.

Significant among the iconographers of the Moscow School was Simon Ushakov. He worked in the Kremlin Chamber of Icons, a major state sponsored icon workshop which also produced other paintings as required by the state. This school was heavily influenced by western art. It introduced a realistic representation of the figures and their surrounds, three dimensional space, and a concept of "divine beauty" – all borrowed from the baroque of Western Europe. While the overall form of the icon was maintained, its meaning and purpose were shifted. These icons were intended not so much for instruction and contemplation, as to impress. It is interesting to compare the complexity of the icon of the Holy Trinity written by Ushakov (see Figure 7.6) with the simplicity of the one written by Rublev. That this school was also required to produce commercial portraits of secular figures was probably one major catalyst for these developments. However, Ushakov also argued strongly that icons should be the best art available and that this was the three dimensional representative art of the west. He considered that foreigners would laugh at Russian art if it continued with the traditional icon style. This westernizing trend was continued when the capital moved to St. Petersburg in 1703. St. Petersburg was very much more cosmopolitan and here icons were painted in oils, and a sensuality was introduced by the use of light and shade.

Figure 7.6
The Holy Trinity Icon by Simon Ushakov of the Moscow school.

As well as the state sponsored workshops, there were also other private icon workshops sponsored by families such as the Stroganovs. The Stroganovs were a wealthy merchant family who effectively ruled a large part of Russia from their seat in Solvychegodsk. The Stroganov Icon School produced small, precious icons of the saints. These were family devotional icons, mainly representing the name patrons of members of the family. This is the sophisticated art of a wealthy class and the military saints in particular are painted in a delicate, affected style.

There were two forces which reacted against the westernizing influences in Russian iconography. These were the monastic workshops and the community of the Old Ritualists (or Old Believers). As in most Orthodox countries, monasteries formed an important part of Russian iconography from the beginning. They were less influenced by outside artist fashions and retained a purer iconographic style. As Onasch and Schnieper say:

> They retained the obligatory visual patterns set down by the painter's manuals for a longer period than did their secular rivals. Even after they had cautiously opened up to the spirit of the times, icons from this source kept their traditional structural patterns as well as the liturgically determined choice of colours, and also a stubborn insistence on reverse perspective, the indispensable "door to the world of the spirit.[77]

The Old Ritualists (or Old Believers) come from a split in the Russian Church over the reforms introduced by Patriarch Nikon in the late seventeenth century. The Old Believers refused to accept these reforms and sought to preserve ancient church forms, including the form of the icons. This was a persecuted movement and the icon schools were mostly village-based craft communities, although there were some monasteries in the far north. The best-known of these village schools were Palekh, Cholui and Mstera, where icon guilds developed.

The final word on the Russian tradition should perhaps be given to its most enthusiastic promoter: Leonid Ouspensky.

> The Russian Icon is the highest expression in art of godlike humility. This is why, in spite of its extremely deep meaning, it has a child-like lightness and joy and is full of tranquil peace and warmth. Having come into contact through Byzantium with the traditions of the ancient world…Russian iconography was not fascinated by the charm of this inheritance. It uses it only as a means, introduces it completely into the church, and transfigures it; and thus the beauty of antique art acquires its true meaning in the transfigured countenance of the Russian Icon.[78]

---

[77] Onasch and Schnieper, *Icons: The Fascination and the Reality*, 96.
[78] Ouspensky and Lossky, *The Meaning of Icons*, 45.

The Border Kingdoms

The interaction of icons and western art was most intense in those countries in the border regions between eastern and western Christianity. In countries such as Romania and the Ukraine, regions such as Galicia, islands such as Cyprus and Crete and in the empire of Venice, there was a complex artistic interaction. It would be wrong to think that the influence was all one way – western art contaminating traditional icons. Traditional iconography had a big influence on western art, particularly through the use of immigrant Byzantine artists in Venice. Thus, Giotto's painting of the stigmata of St. Francis follows the pattern of a traditional icon, with a stylized landscape, compressed perspective and gold background, even though its subject comes solidly from the Western tradition. Likewise, in Caravaggio's painting of the Death of the Virgin, in every way a classic late renaissance painting, Mary is dressed in red and a red cloth is draped across the background – both clear references to traditional iconography.

The Western influence on the icons of the border regions was, however, more profound. It involved the use of non-traditional materials. Thus, in Bohemia, icons were painted onto glass, and incorporated non-traditional elements or subjects. So it is that from Venice we have a traditional icon of the Dormition of Mary, but with Saints Francis and Dominic standing at the sides. The art of these border regions often shows more realistic and expressive faces, replacing the Byzantine aloofness, and more detailed backgrounds. The art of the crusader kingdoms are superb examples of this.

One particular example is worth mentioning: the icon of Our lady of Perpetual Succour (see Figure 7.7). This icon was originated in Crete and is a variant of the "loving kindness" icons. It has all the hallmarks of the border icons – the faces are expressive and the humanity of Christ is evident. In Russia, this pattern is known as "the Mother of the Passion." The original icon was taken to Rome, where it still resides, and it became one of the most popular and reproduced of all icons. For many years, it was the only traditional icon known to Latin Catholics, and it became the centre of a widespread devotional cult. This is still, by far, the most popular icon in the West.

Figure 7.7
The Icon of Our Lady of Perpetual Succour

The Oriental Churches

Coptic art is predominately the Christian art of the upper Nile valley of Egypt. It reached its mature phase in the late fifth and sixth centuries. The development of Coptic art was interrupted by the Arab Islamic conquest of Egypt between 640 and 642 CE. Its subsequent course was marked by iconoclastic Islamic influences and a repetition of earlier forms. In contrast with the aristocratic taste prevailing in cosmopolitan Alexandria, which was in close touch with the leading artistic centres of the Roman Empire, older and deeply ingrained traditions remained in force in the upper Nile valley, where an intensely religious culture drew its following chiefly from the lower classes. Coptic art is characterized by a high degree of stylization verging on abstraction (see Figure 7.8). Forms are flattened out, and individual motifs acquire bold simplicity and decorative character.[79]

---

[79] *The Columbia Electronic Encyclopaedia*, 6th ed. Columbia University Press, 2004.

Figure 7.8
Coptic Icon of Christ and Saint Peter

The Armenian and Syrian churches were deeply suspicious of the Byzantine veneration of images. This was mostly because of their support for the teachings of Nestrorius on the incarnation and the nature of Christ. In particular, Armenian theologians rejected the notion that icons are a medium of direct, or sacramental, representation. This suspicion of images was so great that the churches of the Syro-Malabar Rite, an oriental church in communion with Rome, had to be instructed to include images in their churches.

Ethiopian

One particular church which needs to be discussed is the Ethiopian. This is an ancient Christian church which retains a strong connectedness with ancient Judaism. Almost all of the early imagery of this church, which was probably in the Coptic style, has been lost. This is due to the iconoclastic fervor which influenced it from Byzantium, as well as to persistent Islamic influences. The medieval art of Ethiopia shows strong Byzantine influences although with African elements such as giraffes and antelopes. These early works also show a strong Islamic influence with complicated geometric and decorative patterns. The Byzantine influence declined after the fall of Byzantium, with Coptic and Arab models starting to dominate. Other influences include Indian art through trade contacts, and Western European art through Italian and Portuguese travelers. To all of these influences the Ethiopians brought their own austere style. In the seventeenth century, the

Jesuits had a major influence on the iconography of Ethiopia by introducing prints of Western European art. The typical Ethiopian Madonna, for example, is clearly modeled on a picture of the Virgin Mary in St. Mary Major in Rome. Owing to the relative poverty of the Ethiopian church, gold leaf in the background in often replaced with yellow paint, giving a very distinctive colour palette to the Ethiopian icons (see Figure 7.9).

Figure 7.9
Ethiopian Icon of St. George.

The Celts

Another distinctive tradition which we need to discuss, even if only to mourn its loss, is that of the Celts. Here we are talking essentially about the Irish church, since the other Celtic areas had all come under the dominion of Rome. The Irish iconographic tradition is interesting because it comes from a non-imaging culture which adopted figurative art with Christianity. This is in stark contrast to classical civilization which had to Christianize its strong tradition of figurative art. Unfortunately, most of this Celtic tradition is lost to us because of the violent history of Ireland. This includes particularly the raids of the Vikings, who would destroy anything which they didn't recognized as being of value, such as books and paintings, and the savage iconoclasm of the Protestant English, which was particularly savage in Ireland because it was connected to the political attempt to suppress Irish nationality and religion.

That the Irish did adopt iconographic art we only know from the few remnants that survive. Cormac's Chapel at Cashel was once covered with mosaics. Just enough remains to show that they were brilliantly coloured and also deliberately chipped off. The intricately carved High Cross was a feature of many Irish monasteries and seems to have been a catechetical tool.

The most complete record left to us of the Irish Iconography is in the illuminated manuscripts which are, ironically, better preserved and more numerous in Continental Europe than they are in Ireland. The most famous of these is the Book of Kells which is preserved in Trinity College, Dublin (see Figure 7.10). The illuminations of these documents are highly distinctive. There is a maze of complex geometric decoration, animals and plants are highly stylized and merged into the geometric pattern. Human figures are rare, but where they exist they are also highly stylized and lack any sense of realism. The eyes are noticeably prominent. This combination of highly stylized figures with prominent eyes is very reminiscent of Coptic art, and an eastern influence in the early Irish church is not impossible. However, there was clearly no tradition of the "true image." Christ is portrayed with blue eyes, red beard and blond, wavy hair. The apostles are shown with red hair. All of this suggests an independent and indigenous origin.

Figure 7.10
Image of Christ and Two Apostles from the Book of Kells

The loss of the Celtic tradition of iconography is not just the regrettable loss of another cultural view. Celtic spirituality placed great emphasis on God imminent in nature as opposed to a transcendent emphasis in the Byzantine tradition. Jesus

Christ was seen to be incarnate in the natural world – a vital insight for a global society faced with environmental degradation. We have this spirituality preserved in traditional prayers as can be seen in the excerpts given below:

St Ciaran's Prayer[80]

O star like sun, O guiding light, O home of planets
O fiery manned and marvelous one,
O fertile, undulating fiery-sea
Forgive…

St Patrick's Breastplate[81]

I arise today through the strength of heaven,
Light of sun, radiance of moon,
Splendor of fire, speed of lightening,
Swiftness of wind, depth of sea,
Stability of rock, firmness of earth….

Carmina Gadelica[82]

There is no plant in the ground
But is full of his virtue.
There is no form in the strand
But is full of his blessing….

There is no life in the sea
There is no creature in the river
There is naught in the firmament
But proclaims his goodness…

There is no bird on the wing,
There is no star in the sky,
There is nothing beneath the sun
But proclaims his goodness….

We have the words of the Celts but, for the great part, their images, which could have spoken to our hearts, are lost to us.

---

[80] T. Joyce, *Celtic Christianity: Sacred Tradition, a Vision of Hope* (Maryknoll, NY: Orbis, 1998), 142.

[81] Many different translations. This one is based on T. Cahill, *How the Irish saved Civilization: The Untold Story of Ireland's Heroic Role from the Fall of Rome to the Rise of Medieval Europe* (London: Hodder and Stoughton, 1995), 116.

[82] Cited in Ian Bradley, *Celtic Christian Communities: Live the Tradition* (Kelowana, British Columbia, Canada: Northstone Publishing, 2000), 72.

CHAPTER EIGHT

WRITING THE ICON

Icons have been created in the Orthodox Church in order to externalize the sacred tradition and to enable us who approach them to enter into the unseen world of the Spirit, there we can experience the power of divine grace healing and restoring us to the image and likeness of God. The iconographer, who is engaged in "the heavenly task given by God" of externalizing the sacred tradition in the language of sacred art, where every line and every colour has a meaning, undertakes the "writing" of the icon in a contemplative atmosphere of prayer. In following the tradition and the artistic rules and conventions of iconography, the iconographer brings the sacred and divine mysteries of the faith before the eyes of the believers for their contemplation; draws them past the image to the prototype; and brings them into contact with a tradition of Christian spirituality where inner stillness, attentiveness and recollection, lie at the very heart of the life of the Church.[83] The iconographer's engagement in God's task is not that of a creative artist, but of an instrument in the hands of God, participating in a spiritual journey of prayer. [84]

The Visual Language of Icons

As we enter a world where the silence of the non-verbal symbolic language of form and colour draws us to gaze at the icon in thoughtful contemplation, we discover that we are not looking at a naturalistic work of art. In the stillness of our contemplation we gradually discover that we are receiving "the gaze of the One who looks back at us, knowing us and loving us to a newfound transformation."[85] The stillness and inner recollection that many icons convey is brought about partly through the use of geometric forms, which create a sense of harmony and order. In icons that depict Christ the Savior as the King of Glory, for example (see Figure 8.1), Christ is surrounded by the shape of a dark oval mandorla and a red diamond and rectangle which form an octagonal star. The majestic figure of Christ is placed within a red diamond enclosed in the mandorla. In the corners of the red rectangle, traced beyond the mandorla, are the symbols of the evangelists receiving rays of light from Christ who is in the centre of the icon. This technique of the combination of geometric shapes, not only "centres" the whole composition, but draws us "into the harmony and balance of the icon of Him in whom 'all things hold together'" (Col 1:17).[86] In other icons a sense of harmony and balance is achieved through the use of a triangular pattern, or a circle hidden within the icon, to keep the various elements together.

---

[83] Baggley, *Doors of Perception*, 1, 55-56.

[84] H.Gerhard, *The World of Icons* (London: John Murray, 1971), 211.

[85] Cited in "March 2012 Prayer and Reflection" http://www.catholicdigest.com/articles/food_fun/catholic_art/2012/02-15/march-2012-prayer-and-reflection [accessed 1 November, 2012]. See also, Baggley, *Doors of Perception*, 78-79.

[86] Baggley, *Doors of Perception*, 80. See also, Ouspensky and Lossky, *The Meaning of Icons*, 72-73.

Figure 8.1
The King of Glory

In order to show that the icon refers to the unseen world of the Spirit, the technique of *inverse perspective* is often employed. In many icons the lines of perspective do not converge towards a vanishing point within the scene, as they do in an ordinary painting, but they diverge into endless space "behind" the icon, leading our thoughts towards an existence that never ends.[87] Leonid Ouspensky, in his *Theology of the Icon*, explains that

> Inverse perspective is not an 'optical illusion.' It does not fascinate the spectator and lead [one] into a futile game of appearances. On the contrary, it calms [one], makes [one] concentrate, and makes [one] attentive to the message of the icon. It is as if [one] were standing before a path which, instead of losing itself in space, opens onto infinite fullness.[88]

In following the lines of inverse perspective in the opposite direction, we find that the lines converge in the eyes of the beholder. This technique gives the impression that the persons or events represented in the icon are not only looking at us, but are

[87]   Solrunn Nes, *The Mystical Language of Icons* (London: St Paul's, 2000), 20. See also, Baggley, *Doors of Perception*, 80-81; Paul Evdokimov, *The Art of the Icon: A Theology of Beauty* (Redondo Beach, CA: Oakwood, 1972), 225.
[88]   Ouspensky, *Theology of the Icon*, 225.

actually coming out to greet us. In this way a communion is established between the persons or event depicted in the icon and ones self.[89]

In many icons the figures are noticeably out of scale when compared to the surroundings. This feature of iconography, known as *hierarchical perspective*, in which the importance of the figure determines its size, leads us to focus our attention on the important elements in the icon.[90] *Curved horizon perspective*, the bending of buildings or objects towards the holy figure in the icon, represents a universe transfigured in the light of Christ.[91] Other deliberate distortions of perspectives give a "view from above, as of God looking down; or from below as of the spectator looking heavenward; or a view from the ground level as if the spectator were prostrate at the feet of the saint."[92] These distortions of perspectives which can be used together with inverse and normal perspectives, can lead us to recognize that the world in which we live is also the scene where the events of the spiritual world are unfolding. In order to

> enter into this [spiritual] world, our minds must be converted, and we must pass through the narrow gate that leads to life (Matthew 7.13-14). Our own perspectives have to be changed as we enter into the realms that the icons open-up for us; communication takes place in the stillness, and the leaving behind of the normal external world leads to the cosmos transfigured in the light of Christ.[93]

The theology of transfiguration, the teaching that the light of the Transfiguration experienced by Peter, James and John (Mt 17:1-8) "was not a created light but was the uncreated light of divine energy," controls the colour and line of an icon.[94] This uncreated light, which is experienced at the deepest level of prayer, transfigures us into God's image "from one degree of glory to another" (2 Cor 3:18) and, through the presence of the saints, it transfigures all of creation.[95] In the words of Ouspensky,

> This ascension of [humankind] reverses the process of the Fall and begins to deliver the universe from disorder and corruption, since the deification attained by the saint constitutes the beginning of the cosmic transfiguration to come.[96]

---

[89] Nes, *The Mystical Language of Icons*, 20. See also, Baggley, *Doors of Perception*, 80-81.
[90] Nes, *The Mystical Language of Icons*, 20, 41, 85.
[91] Guillem Ramos-Poqui, *The Technique of Icon Painting* (Tunbridge Wells, UK: Burns & Oats, 1990) , 54. An example of the use of this technique is seen in the icon *The Raising of Lazarus*, 59.
[92] Ramos-Poqui, *The Technique of Icon Painting*, 54.
[93] Baggley, *Doors of Perception*, 81.
[94] Brentnall, "The Language of Orthodox Icons", 11.
[95] Brentnall, "The Language of Orthodox Icons", 4.
[96] Ouspensky, *Theology of the Icon*, 158. See also the letter of St Paul to the Romans 8:20-21.

The iconographer uses the techniques involved with light and colour to show the world and humanity deified by the light of divine energies (grace).[97] The use of gold (an important symbol of divine energy and transformation) in the background of icons and on halos gives the icon a luminous quality. In addition, the application of liquid gold to parts of the face, clothing, buildings and landscape, in the later stages of "writing" the icon, show a world "completely surrounded and permeated with light."[98] As we look into the illuminated world of the icon we discover that the source of light, which is Light Itself, emanates from within. Unlike our world which has an external source for its light, creating shadows that speak of time and corruption, there are no shadows in the world of the icon. The light of the divine energies transforms buildings, mountains and vegetation, "and is particularly manifested in the inner illumination of the saints." [99]

Other colours used to express the light of divine energies and transfiguration are white, red and purple. In the icons of the *Nativity* (see Figure 8.2) and the *Transfiguration* (see Figure 8.3), white is used to emphasize the divine nature of Christ. Christ is wrapped in white swaddling clothes as an infant, and is clothed in a white garment as he is transfigured on the mountain of Tabor.

Figure 8.2
The Nativity of Christ

Figure 8.3
The Transfiguration

---

[97] Brentnall, "The Language of Orthodox Icons", 11. For a detailed description of colours and their meanings see Michel Quenot, *The Icon: Window on the Kingdom* (Crestwood, New York: St Vladimir's Seminary Press, 1991), 111-119.

[98] Nes, *The Mystical Language of Icons*, 20. See also, Brentnall, "The Language of Orthodox Icons", 12.

[99] Baggley, *Doors of Perception*, 81.

The depiction of Lazarus in a white robe in the icon of the *Raising of Lazarus* (see Figure 8.4) represents the illumination of the New Life bestowed on Lazarus by Christ, the Incarnate Word of God, who became man so that we might be made divine by grace.[100]

Figure 8.4
The Raising of Lazarus

Red, blue and purple are the colours used in Mary's *maphorion* (cloak) to symbolize that she has put on the light of divine grace. The three gold stars on her *maphorion* symbolize her virginity before, during and after giving birth, and highlight her unique position as the mother of the Son of God.[101] In the icons of martyrs, red is used as a symbol, not of their suffering, but of their glory.

Black is used to symbolize "that which is waiting to be transfigured," and can also be used to represent the mystery of God's unknowable essence or divine darkness.[102] In the icons of the *Nativity* (see Figure 8.2) and the *Baptism of Jesus* (see Figure 8.5), the darkness of the world (cave) and the dark waters of the Jordan (depicted in the shape of a cave) are transfigured by Christ's entrance into them. Just as Christ's descent into the world transfigures all matter, so too Christ's descent into the water transfigures all water from a symbol of death and chaos to a symbol of life and renewal. The dark semi-circle at the top of the icons, suffused with golden rays, symbolizes the unfathomable mystery of God. It is dark because God, in God's

---

[100] Brentnall, "The Language of Orthodox Icons", 12, 37. See also, Cross, *Eastern Christianity,* 36.

[101] Nes, *The Mystical Language of Icons,* 45.

[102] Brentnall, "The Language of Orthodox Icons", 12.

essence, is unknowable. It has gold rays because God in His energies can be known and experienced, and "it is by these energies that [God] transfigures creation."[103] The centre of the *mandorla* (the circle of light found in many icons) is often black to symbolize the unknowable essence of God. The movement of the lines in an icon also expresses the theological theme of transfiguration. A good example of the ascension from a dark world to a world of glory, can be clearly seen is in the icon of the Baptism.[104]

Figure 8.5
The Baptism of Jesus

The most noticeable non-naturalistic feature in an icon is the way in which buildings are drawn. In the icon of the *Annunciation* (see Figure 8.6), for instance, one of the pillars is placed directly over a hole in the building behind Mary.[105] Scenes never take place in enclosed walls since the action that takes place is "outside the limits of time and space, that is, everywhere and in front of everyone."[106] In order to indicate that the event took place inside, a red cloth is draped across the buildings. The cloth is a symbol of the "veil which concealed the Holy of Holies in the Old Testament and which is now opened to reveal the Christian message to the world."[107]

[103] Brentnall, "The Language of Orthodox Icons", 35. The language of "essence" and "energies" touches on an older theme which is that of the luminous darkness, that paradox which was used to talk about the mystical encounters with God, that is to be found in the writings of the early Fathers of the Church, particularly in Gregory of Nyssa's *Life of Moses*.
[104] Brentnall, "The Language of Orthodox Icons", 13.
[105] Baggley, *Doors of Perception*, 83.
[106] Evdokimov, *The Art of the Icon*, 224.
[107] Ramos-Poqui, *The Technique of Icon Painting*, 56.

Figure 8.6
Annunciation

The non-naturalistic buildings

> help to show that the event and its significance are not confined
> to a precise historical moment of time and space; they belong to
> the world of the spirit, to a world of human consciousness that
> is richer and more mysterious than the ordinary everyday world
> of rational decisions and logical actions. The wider significance
> of the events portrayed has to be worked out in the soul of those
> who behold the icon; what the icon represents may have been
> manifested at a precise point in time and space, but its fuller
> significance is found in the inner world where the true work of
> purification, illumination, and union have to be accomplished.
> Thus the non-realistic buildings used as the setting in an icon
> can open up to us the awareness that it is our own inner world
> that is being addressed, and to which our attention is being
> directed. The illumination given by a specific event or person
> and set forth in the icon has to be accomplished in our souls
> also.[108]

The distorted geometric outlines of the mountains, and the design of the patterns
of light on the slopes, are represented as if they are leaning towards the saint in an
attitude of respect, signifying that even the environment has been transfigured by

---

[108] Baggley, *Doors of Perception*, 82-83.

the presence of the saint depicted. "Trees and vegetation also acknowledge this presence by bending towards the saint, or bursting forth towards the realm of the divine."[109] Examples of the distorted mountains can be seen in the icons of the *Nativity* (see Figure 8.2), the *Baptism of Jesus* (see Figure 8.5), the *Raising of Lazarus* (see Figure 8.4) and the *Transfiguration* (see Figure 8.3). Since mountains are symbolic of the place where God's presence was manifested, the distorted mountains remind us that the event depicted in the icon "is of one of major spiritual significance."[110]

The iconographer's schematic and stylized portrayal of the human form serves to emphasize "the dematerialized, spiritual form of the [person] transfigured by divine grace."[111] In the icon of *St Nicholas* (see Figure 8.7), for example, the 'distorted' forehead, nose, ears, and mouth convey a "sense of inner concentration of spiritual energies in attentiveness and prayer."[112] The large, staring eyes that "gaze continually at the Lord" (Ps 25:15) because they have seen the Lord's salvation (Lk 2:30) also invite us to participate in the divine life.[113] In leading us to turn our gaze towards the interior life of the Spirit we discover that, in order to experience the presence of divine wisdom (high forehead), to receive the inner light and to be attentive only to the Lord's voice, the doors of the external world of the senses (symbolized by the long, thin nose, small mouth and ears) must be closed.[114]

Figure 8.7
St Nicholas

---

[109] Ramos-Poqui, *The Technique of Icon Painting*, 57. See also, Brentnall, "The Language of Orthodox Icons", 13.

[110] Baggley, *Doors of Perception*, 130. See also, Ramos-Poqui, *The Technique of Icon Painting*, 57.

[111] Baggley, *Doors of Perception*, 83.

[112] Baggley, *Doors of Perception*, 118.

[113] Quenot, *The Icon*, 97.

[114] Brentnall, "The Language of Orthodox Icons", 14. See also, Baggley, *Doors of Perception*, 83.

The depiction of bodies as static or immobile, such as Moses and Elijah in the icon of the *Transfiguration* (see Figure 8.3), is a technique used to suggest that they are spellbound by the presence of the divine, or that the world in which they live is one of inner peace.[115] Mobility, such as that of Peter, James and John seen in the same icon, is used to convey the idea of confusion and agitation. Elongated bodies and lengthy fingers "indicate dematerialization in the most eloquent way, revealing the flow of spiritual intensity flooding forth from those who are portrayed on the icons."[116]

The non-naturalistic shapes of hands and fingers, and their position and gesture in an icon have deep symbolic meaning. In the icons of the *Mother of God of Hodigitria* ('the one who shows the way', see Figure 8.8), Mary's left hand and fingers point towards her Son. This simple gesture of pointing moves our attention to the Incarnate Son of God who is "the Way, the Truth and the Life" (Jn 14:6). This gesture is also common in the icons of the *Presentation of Mary in the Temple* (see Figure 8.9), where the gesture of pointing by Joachim and Anna moves our attention towards Mary.

Figure 8.8
The Mother of God (Theotokos Hodigitria)

---

[115] Brentnall, "The Language of Icons", 13.
[116] Quenot, *The Icon*, 100.

Figure 8.9
The Entry of the Theotokos in the Temple

In icons of *Christ Pantocrator* (see Figure 8.10), Christ's right hand is raised in a gesture of blessing that is turned inwards towards the heart. The way in which the hand is depicted in a gesture of blessing is described by Dionysius of Fourna in his *Painter's Manual* as follows:

> When you paint the blessing hand, do not join the three fingers together, but only cross the thumb and the fourth finger; so that the upright finger, that is to say the index finger, and the bent middle finger denote the name IC since the upright finger denotes the I, and the curved one which is next to it, the C. The thumb and the fourth finger, which are crossed, with the little finger beside it, denote the name XC. Since the oblique part of the fourth finger, from where it meets the middle finger, makes the X sign and the little finger, where it is curved, the C. In this way the name XC is shown, and through the divine providence of the creator of all things the fingers of the hand of mankind are formed in such a way, with neither more nor fewer but as many as are sufficient to signify this name.[117]

This symbol and gesture leads us "into the spirituality of the hesychast tradition,[118]

---

[117] Cited in Baggley, *Doors of Perception*, 84-85. See also, Brentnall, "The Language of Orthodox Icons", 13. The hand of blessing can also "express the Trinity and the two natures of the Chalcedonian Definition."

[118] The peaceful or calm way.

where the Name of Jesus Christ is closely linked with the prayer of the heart."[119] As well as leading us to "embark on the prayer of the heart [the icon] forms the door through which we can enter into that interior work."[120]

Figure 8.10
Christ Pantocrator

The Painting of Icons

The process of creating an icon is a long and complex task involving several different craft techniques, namely: the preparation of the panel; the application of the *gesso* ground (plaster mixed with animal glue); the drafting of the composition; gilding of the background; and the painting. The first stage consists of the preparation of a well-seasoned solid wood panel such as cypress, oak, beech or pine. Some panels need to be strengthened with slats or spleens at the back to prevent them from warping. As the slats or spleens need to be of a harder wood than that of the panel, they often provide useful evidence of the age of the icon. The carving out of a slightly shallow, flat surface in the front of the panel leaves a surrounding border that protects the icon and acts as a partition between that which is holy and the

---

[119] Baggley, *Doors of Perception*, 85.
[120] Baggley, *Doors of Perception*, 85.

ordinary world. One practical advantage of raised borders is that a ruler or piece of wood may be placed across the icon to allow the hand to be supported during painting.[121]

When the wood panel is ready it is coated several times with *glue size*[122] which penetrates and seals the wood. Before the final coat dries, the panel is covered with a thin piece of loosely woven linen. Air pockets and wrinkles are removed by firmly pressing the glue-soaked linen on the surface using one's fingers or a damp cloth. As soon as the linen has been pressed firmly onto the base, it is coated over straight away with more *size*, so that it is well saturated, and then left to dry. The linen serves as an under-layer for the *gesso* ground on which the icon is to be "written." This under-layer is very important because it holds the ground more firmly to the panel, protects the panel from splitting, and prevents the ground from peeling off once the panel begins to warp. When the under-layer is completely dry, a number of layers of the *gesso* grounding are applied, each of which must be completely dried, cleaned, and sanded down to a smooth finish.

While the *gesso* is drying, the iconographer uses the help of other icons, or iconographic manuals or handbooks, to prepare a basic sketch of the composition of the icon. After the drawing is transferred to the gessoed panel, either by using tracing paper or sketching directly onto it with a pencil or tempera colour, the iconographer incises the lines of the drawing with a sharp tool such as a needle (*stylus*) or a long sharpened nail. This method, which requires great patience and exactness, allows the outlines of the composition to be seen through the paint during work.[123]

Once the outlines of the composition are transferred to the smooth gessoed panel, a decision needs to be made whether to gild (work with gold leaf) or paint the background of the icon.[124] Of the two methods of gilding, water gilding and oil gilding, the most effective is water gilding. This gilding technique, the oldest and most time consuming, makes it possible for the gold leaf to be burnished to reflect the light, making it appear as if it was solid gold. The first step involves spreading several coats of bole (soft clay mixed with animal glue) smoothly over the background area where the gold leaf will be placed. After the boled surface has dried, it is rubbed with the finest steel wool, fine emery paper and agate stone until its surface is absolutely smooth. This is most necessary as any scratch or fault will show through the gold leaf when it is applied.

---

[121] Nes, *The Mystical Language of Icons*, 8. See also, Ramos-Poqui, *The Technique of Icon Painting*, 18; John Stuart, *Ikons* (London: Faber & Faber, 1975), 41; Ouspensky and Lossky, *The Meaning of Icons*, 53.

[122] Glue size is a combination of water and animal glue. Fish glue or gelatine may also be used See Nes, *The Mystical Language of Icons*, 8 and Ramos-Poqui, The *Technique of Icon Painting*, 19 for more detailed information on the making and the application of glue size to the panel.

[123] Ouspensky and Lossky, *The Meaning of Icons*, 53-54. See also, Nes, The *Mystical Language of Icons* , 8; Ramos-Poqui, *The Technique of Icon Painting*, 21-22.

[124] Nes, *The Mystical Language of Icons*, 9.

Each piece of gold leaf is placed on a gilder's cushion and is cut to shape with a special knife. It is then lifted with a slightly greasy and "static" gilder's tip and laid carefully on the boled surface, which has been brushed over several times with a solution of thinned animal glue and technical spirit. This solution will cement the gold leaf to the boled surface. After a short time, the gold is burnished systematically with an agate burnisher. The more it is burnished, and the greater the increase of pressure, the more the gold will shine. The oil gilding technique involves the use of an oil-based, slow drying glue and the transfer of sheets of gold leaf, that are stuck on to sheets of paper, by rubbing. Whilst this technique is the simplest of the two, it is not as effective since, due to the matt finish, the gold cannot be burnished. Instead of using gold leaf for the gold background, the gold background can be painted by hand with egg tempera, a mixture of egg yolk, water and coloured pigments.[125]

Once the background is gilded, the actual painting or "writing" of the icon begins. The painting is built up from darker (cooler) tones to lighter (warmer) tones of colour in definite consecutive stages. The first painting stage involves the application of the base colour to all the areas of the icon. This may be done either by flooding the paint onto the panel ('*petit lac*' method)[126] with well-loaded "rigger" brushes, or by applying the paint in thin coats with flat brushes. In stage two, "the original drawing of the icon is re-traced, along the incised principal lines and outlines with a darker tone of the same [base] colour."[127] In the third painting stage, the first layer of lights is applied. Once this is completed all the painted areas (not the gold background) are coated with a transparent "nourishing layer" of egg yolk/water solution that "binds" all the layers of colour together.[128] The fourth and final stage involves the painting of "letters, halos and gold lines, final build-up of layers of light and slight deepening of shadow areas, reinforcement of lines, final details and highlights."[129] The positioning of the lettering on the panel, which is a reference either to the event or to the saint's name, "is planned as an integral part of the whole composition."[130] It is the inscription on the icon which gives it its presence.[131] After several months the icon is varnished, and then taken to the church for a blessing.[132]

Iconography renders an immense service to the Church by revealing, in a unique pictorial language, the spiritual world of humanity as transfigured, by the light of divine energies, into the image of Christ. Through the use of colours, forms, lines

---

[125] Ramos-Poqui, *The Technique of Icon Painting*, 22, 44-47. See also, Nes, *The Mystical Language of Icons*, 9-10.
[126] For a more detailed description of this method see Ramos-Poqui, *The Technique of Icon Painting*, 26, 31.
[127] Ouspensky and Lossky, *The Meaning of Icons*, 54.
[128] Ramos-Poqui, *The Technique of Icon Painting*, 33.
[129] Ramos-Poqui, The *Technique of Icon Painting*, 30. The details of this stage are discussed on page 34.
[130] Stuart, *Ikons*, 49.
[131] Brentnall, "The Language of orthodox Icons", 14.
[132] The icon has to stand for several months before varnishing because it takes a long time for the egg painting medium to harden thoroughly. For a detailed description of varnishing and the mounting of the icon see Ramos-Poqui, The *Technique of Icon Painting*, 50.

and expressions, icons announce the Good News of the Gospel; that God has come among us, as one of us, to call us to "become participants in the divine nature" (2 Pet 1:4).

> The implications of this new destiny offered to all who have 'put
> on Christ' (Gal 3:27) concern not only human beings who are thus
> reinstated in their royal dignity and office, but also the whole of
> creation which is re-created in Christ and called to renewal and
> transfiguration through the deification of humanity.[133]

Icons orient our total being towards transfiguration and at the same time they help us to

> decipher every human face as an icon. For every human face
> is an icon. Beneath all the masks, all the ashes, every human
> being, however ravaged he or she may be by his or her destiny,
> by the destiny of history and civilization, carries within him or
> her the pearl of great price, this hidden face.[134]

Iconography assists us in our pursuit of holiness in our everyday lives by reminding us that, in our journey towards perfection, we are not alone. We are accompanied and sustained by Christ, the Mother of God, and all the saints.[135]

---

[133] G.Limouris, "Introductory Note", in *Icons. Windows on Eternity,* ed. G.Limouris (Geneva: WCC Publications, 1990), ix.

[134] G.Limouris, "The Microcosm and Macrocosm of the Icon: Theology, Spirituality and Worship in Colour," in *Icons. Windows on Eternity,* ed. G.Limouris (Geneva: WCC Publications, 1990), 118-119.

[135] Limouris, "The Microcosm," 116.

CHAPTER NINE

FIXED GREAT FEASTS OF THE BYZANTINE LITURGICAL YEAR

In the Byzantine Church there are Twelve Great or Major Feasts which consist of nine fixed feasts which are celebrated on the same dates each year and three moveable feasts which depend on the date of Pascha or Easter. The nine fixed Great Feasts are: The Nativity of the Theotokos (8 September); The Exaltation of the Cross (14 September); The Entry of the Theotokos into the Temple (21 November); The Nativity of Christ (25 December); Theophany or The Baptism of Jesus (6 January); The Holy Meeting of Our Lord or The Presentation of Jesus in the Temple (2 February); The Annunciation (25 March); The Transfiguration of Our Lord (6 August); The Dormition of the Theotokos (15 August). The three moveable Great Feasts are: Palm Sunday; The Ascension and Pentecost. The Byzantine Liturgical Year begins on 1 September and ends on 31 August of the following year. There are also other feasts, such as the Protection of the Mother of God (Pokrov- The Protecting Veil), which whilst not numbered amongst the twelve Great Feasts, are none the less important.

The Eastern Church begins its year with the Nativity of the Theotokos as its first Great Feast and ends its year with its last Great Feast the Dormition of the Theotokos. Thus the Church begins and ends the year with Mary the Theotokos, Mother of God.

The Nativity of the Theotokos, Mother of God (8 September)

> *Your Nativity, O Mother of God,*
> *heralded joy to the whole universe,*
> *for from you rose the Sun of Justice,*
> *Christ our God.*
> *He canceled the curse and poured forth his grace:*
> *He vanquished death and granted us eternal life.* [136]

The feast of the Nativity of the Theotokos is the first major feast of the Byzantine calendar. It is celebrated on 8 September, and commemorates Mary's place in the great work of Redemption. The Orthodox Church invites us to celebrate the "prelude of universal joy and the first fruits of our salvation."[137]

The feast of the Nativity of the Blessed Virgin Mary, one of the oldest of the Marian solemnities, was mentioned by the Church Fathers, such as St. Epiphanius and St. John Chrysostom, in the early fifth century. Like other Marian feasts, it began to be celebrated at local level without any major solemnity. As the feast began to spread

---

[136] Joseph Raya and Baron Jose De Vinck, *Byzantine Daily Worship* (Allendale,N.J.: Alleluia Press, 1969), 438.

[137] Michael Evdokimov, *Light from the East: Icons in Liturgy and Prayer* (New York: Paulist Press, 2004), 2; See also, Raya and De Vinck, *Byzantine Daily Worship*, 437.

throughout the Byzantine world in the sixth and seventh century, it was celebrated with greater solemnity. The solemnity of the feast spread to Rome in the seventh century, and in following centuries it spread throughout the whole Western Church. In the eighth century, at the time of St Andrew of Crete (c. 660-740 CE), the feast of Mary's Nativity was already observed and celebrated in the same way as that of other major liturgical feasts of the Byzantine Church. The feast was established on 8 September because it was on that day that St. Helen, Emperor Constantine's mother, dedicated the basilica she built in Jerusalem to the Nativity of the Blessed Virgin Mary.[138]

The *Protoevangelium (Protevangelion) of St James*, an early Christian manuscript dating from the middle of the second century, recounts the nativity and early life of the Blessed Virgin Mary.[139] According to the story, Mary's parents, Joachim and Anne (Anna), were righteous and devout servants of God. They experienced great sadness in their lives because they had not been blessed with children.[140] Their prayers for a child remained unanswered for many years. One day, when Joachim brought his offering to the Temple, Reuben the High priest rejected Joachim's offering and turned him away because Joachim had no children. Greatly distressed by these reproaches, Joachim "retired into the wilderness" to hide his shame. As Joachim opened his heart in prayer to God in the desert, it happened that his wife Anne was praying at the same moment in her garden at their home in Jerusalem. She prayed to the Lord, saying:

> O God of my fathers, bless me and regard my prayer as you did bless the womb of Sarah, and gave her a son, Isaac … what womb did bear me, that I should thus be accursed before the children of Israel, and that they should reproach and deride me in the temple of my God?[141]

While Joachim and Anne were praying at their respective places, an angel of the Lord appeared to both of them and announced that Anne shall conceive and give birth to a child whose name will "be spoken of in all the world."[142] Anne promised to dedicate her child to the Lord. Joachim hurried home with the joyous news and when Anne saw him coming, she too rushed to meet him to share with him the joyous news. As they met at the city gate Anne said, "'Now I know that the Lord

---

[138] Onasch and Schneiper, *Icons*, 148.

[139] Although the *Protevangelium* is not recognized as the inspired Word of God, as is Holy Scripture, much of what it writes about belongs to the tradition of the early Church. See, "The Nativity of the Blessed Virgin Mary" http://www.byzantines.net/SaintAthanasius/tract58.htm. [accessed 2 October, 2004] , 1. See also, Mother Mary and Archimandrite Kallistos Ware, trans., *The Festal Menaion* (London: Faber and Faber, 1977), 47.

[140] "In the Old Testament when God blessed His Chosen people, He always promised to bless them with numerous offspring. Thus, among the Jews, childlessness was considered a sign of God's rejection, a public disgrace (Lk 1:15)." See, *The Nativity, 1*.

[141] *The Protevangelion* http://www.pseudepigrapha.com/LostBooks/protevangelion.htm. [accessed 3 October, 2004], 2.

[142] *The Protevangelion*, 2.

has greatly blessed me; for behold, I who was a widow am no longer a widow, and I who was barren shall conceive.'"[143] As time went on, Joachim and Anne had a baby daughter, whom they called Mary.

The icon of the Nativity of the Mother of God (see Figure 9.1) shows Mary's mother, Anne, resting on a couch, surrounded by two maidservants who are attending to her. Anne is looking towards the lower right of the icon where Mary, wrapped in swaddling clothes, is shown in the lap of a midwife who sits on a stool near a basin filled with water. Mary's representation in swaddling clothes is similar to that of the representation of her soul that appears in the hands of her Son in the Dormition icon. A second midwife is shown pouring the bathwater for the newborn child. There are several variations of the position and attitude of Joachim, Anne's husband. On this icon, Joachim is shown looking out the window of his house. The piece of cloth that hangs between the two buildings anticipates the duty of vestment-maker to the high priest that Mary was to carry out in the Temple. The cloth also appears in the icon of the Annunciation. The abstract architectural houses in the background suggest that the Nativity of the Mother of God is taking place inside the building.[144]

Figure 9.1
Nativity of the Theotokos

The following liturgical texts of the feast of the Nativity of the Theotokos express the spiritual significance of this feast to Orthodox Christians:

---

[143] *The Protevangelion*, 2.
[144] K.Parry, "Nativity of the Mother of God," in *The Blackwell Dictionary of Eastern Christianity*, ed. Ken Parry et al. (Oxford, UK: Blackwell Publishers, 2000), 338-339; See also,.Ouspensky and Lossky, *The Meaning of Icons*, 146; Onasch and Schneiper, *Icons*, 148.

Today Anne the barren one gives birth to the maiden of God who had been chosen from all human generations to become the dwelling place of the Creator, Christ our God and King of all. In her He fulfilled his divine plan through which our human nature was renewed and by which we were to be transferred from corruption to eternal life (Vespers, Tone 6).[145]

What is this sound of feasting that we hear? Joachim and Ann mystically keep festival. 'O Adam and Eve,' they cry, 'rejoice with us today: for if by your transgression ye closed the gate of Paradise to those of old, we have now been given a glorious fruit, Mary the Child of God, who opens its entrance to us all.' (Great Vespers, Tone 2).[146]

The Exaltation of the Cross (14 September)

Hail, precious Cross, guide for the blind, physician of the sick, resurrection of all who have died. You raised us when we fell into corruption. By you did corruption cease and immortality flower forth; by you have we, mortal though we are, been divinised, and the Devil defeated.[147]

The festival of the Exaltation of the Cross recalls a number of related incidents. They are, in chronological order: Constantine's vision of the Cross in 312 CE; the Dedication of the Basilica of the Resurrection in Jerusalem in 335 CE; the finding of the True Cross around the year 340 CE in the city of Jerusalem; and finally, the ceremony of the Raising of the Cross in Constantinople in 629 CE.[148] The feast then celebrates these four events that span across more than three hundred years.

The effect of the appearance of the Cross to Constantine in the year 312 CE was not only Constantine's defeat of his enemy, Maxentius, but also during the following year the Emperor established freedom of religion throughout the Roman Empire. Idol worship was thus defeated and the Church was able to emerge from the era of the catacombs.[149]

The second incident recalled is the Dedication of the Basilica of the Resurrection (the Anastasis), erected by Constantine on the site of the Holy Sepulchre in Jerusalem. This festival of the Dedication was soon associated with yet another incident: the discovery of the True Cross.[150] When Eusebius described the dedication ceremony

---

[145] Raya and De Vinck, *Byzantine Daily Worship*, 440.
[146] Mary and Ware, *The Festal Menaion*, 105.
[147] Evdokimov, *Light from the East*, 11.
[148] Mary and Ware, *Festal Menaion*, 50-51.
[149] Evdokimov, *Light from the East*, 7-8.
[150] Ouspensky and Lossky, *The Meaning of Icons*, 148.

of 335 CE, he does not mention the discovery of the Cross. However, St. Cyril of Jerusalem, writing shortly after Eusebius in 347 CE, declares: "Already the whole universe is filled with fragments of the Wood of the Cross."[151] It is therefore reasonable to conclude that the finding of the Cross must have taken place shortly after the Dedication, around 340 CE. The Cross of Christ was discovered by the mother of Constantine, the Empress Helena, who presented it to St. Macarius, the bishop of Jerusalem, for veneration by the whole world.[152]

Some fifty five years later in 395 CE, St John Chrysostom [153]mentions that the Empress Helena discovered three crosses beneath the mound of Golgotha, and at the the beginning of the fifth century, miracles are attributed to the true cross recognised by St. Helena and St. Macarius. Also, Aetheria[154] the pilgrim nun, in an account of her journey around the year 400, tells us that the festival of the Dedication was celebrated with great solemnity "because the Cross of the Lord was discovered on that day."

> The festival of the Cross was soon to eclipse almost wholly that of the Dedication. In the VIth century, Alexander the Monk speaks of the annual celebration, on September 14, of the Dedication and of the Elevation of the Venerable Cross ... The Basilian menology (ms. at the end of the Xth century) recounts that the day following the Dedication, in 335, the people were admitted for the first time to the contemplation of the sacred wood: the bishop, standing on a height, raised the Cross, to the cries of the faithful, 'Kyrie eleison' ... On September 14th, 614, this rite was performed for the first time in Constantinople. Reconquered from the Persians by the Emperor Heraclius III, the Cross was to be received in triumph at the capital of the Empire, in 628. It was to be brought there finally in 633: the Patriarch Sergius carried it in procession from Blachernes to St Sophia, where the ceremony of the Raising was celebrated with great pomp.[155]

From Constantinople the festival spread to other centres of Christianity. It was celebrated at Rome under Pope Sergius (687 CE – 701 CE), by which time the feast of the Dedication was separated from the feast of the Exaltation.[156] Their feast days are now 13 and 14 September respectively.

---

[151] Catechism 4, 10; P.G. 33, col. 469.
[152] Evdokimov, *Light from the East*, 8.
[153] On St John, Homily 85, 1; P.G.59, col. 461.
[154] Itinerarium Aetheriae, 48-49, ed. Sources chretiennes (Paris, 1948), 262-266.
[155] Ouspensky and Lossky, The Meaning of Icons, 148.
[156] Ouspensky and Lossky, *The Meaning of Icons*, 148.

> O Lord, save your people and bless your inheritance. Give
> victory to those who do battle with evil, and with your Cross, O
> Lord, protect us all.[157]

The icon economically celebrates these events of the Cross (see Figure 9.2). Our attention is skilfully drawn to the Cross, held high by Bishop Macarius. Its features include the distinctive manner Eastern Christianity represents the Cross on which Our Lord was crucified.[158] Above, there is often a short horizontal bar representing the inscription that Pilate placed on the Cross: "Jesus of Nazareth King of the Jews". Then there are the arms of the cross itself, and below is a shorter (usually diagonal) bar, that serves as a footrest. If on a diagonal, it is higher on the right side, near the good thief and sinks lower on the left side toward the unrepentant thief. This diagonal bar is called "the balance of justice" because it resembles the arms of a scale.[159]

Figure 9.2
The Exaltation of the Cross

A deacon, each one sometimes holding a lighted candle, stands on each side of the bishop. The bishop of Jerusalem, standing in front of the Church of the Resurrection, is presenting the Holy Cross for the veneration of the faithful.

---

[157] Evdokimov *Light from the East*, 12.
[158] Evdokimov *Light from the East*, 8.
[159] Evdokimov, *Light from the East*, 9.

> The Cross is raised upon "the place of the skull (Jn 19:17), or
> Golgotha, in which Tradition sees symbolised the centre of the
> world and the burial place of Adam. The Cross is at once the
> instrument and the sign through which Christ, the New Adam,
> frees the cosmos from the darkness of death and grants its
> transfiguration.[160]

The architecture shows that the veneration of the Cross is something done by
and for the Church. Constantine, with his mother Empress Helena by his side, is
pointing towards the Cross that changed the history of the world.

There is a fast prescribed for this feast, as there is for all feasts associated with
the Passion of Our Lord. However, there is a sense of joy and celebration which
accompanies the penitential aspect.[161] Indeed, as the Matins prayer says; "Through
the Cross, joy comes into the world,"

On the Feast of the Holy Cross the whole world is blessed by the raising and
lowering of the cross to the four cardinal points of the earth.[162] The Church signifies
by this rite that the mystery of the Cross redeems the whole world. As men and
women turn their suffering and hopeful eyes toward it, they pray "Before your
Cross, we prostrate ourselves O Lord, and we glorify of your Resurrection."[163]

The veneration of the Cross is an invitation to practice penance and to mediate on
the sufferings of Christ, through which we have redemption. To be a disciple of
Christ means taking up that cross (Matt 10:38). Our cross leads us to where we
wish to go; it points us to God.[164] We submit ourselves to God's justice. It marks
our rebellion against the Christ who died on the Cross, and it marks the moments
when we have accepted the Cross, when we are near enough to hear Our Lord say
"Today you will be with me in paradise (Lk 23:33)."[165]

> Today the Cross is raised on high and all the world shares in its
> saving power, for you who are enthroned with the Father and
> the Holy Spirit have spread your arms upon it and drawn the
> world to know you. By your holy Cross, O Christ, enlighten us
> and save us.[166]

---

[160] Quenot, *The Icon*, 62.
[161] Evdokimov, *Light from the East*, 7.
[162] Evdokimov, *Light from the East*, 8.
[163] Evdokimov, *Light from the East*, 8.
[164] Evdokimov, *Light from the East*, 9.
[165] Evdomikov, *Light from the East*, 9.
[166] Evdokimov, *Light from the East*, 12.

The Protecting Veil of the Mother of God, 'Pokrov'. (1 October)

The Syrian Byzantine Connection

In both the famous Akathistos Hymn and in the poetry St Romanos the Melodist, bothe the work of Syrian Byzantine hymnographers, the most important of all Marian themes is given prominence. Though present in other and earlier works, these two authors emphasise Mary's role in the redemption, associating her closely with Christ. Some would find it uncomfortable to hear the Akathistos Hymn hail her as the *'reconciliation of many sinners,'* the *'stole of those stripped of the right to appeal'* or as the one by whom *'was paid the ransom for transgression.'* When she is hailed as *'gate of salvation'* and as one *'who has begotten anew those who were born in sin,'* the latter-day Christian iconoclast would cry 'Mariolatry!' but mistakenly. The Hymn has been influenced by Apocryphal 'Matthew' and certainly seems to attribute powers to Mary that strictly belong to God, but only because she is 'Theotokos,' mother of the Creator. Also, the 'chairetismoi,' the verses beginning 'hail,' are a special genre whose epithets describing and praising the Virgin are not meant to be exact theological statements. The sole author of man's salvation is the Holy Trinity in Jesus Christ, yet the Virgin plays a unique instrumental role, alike to no one, short of the Godhead itself. In praising her the Byzantine (Syrian) poet seeks to please the Deity, to whom she is not only instrumentally essential in the work of salvation, but to whom she is also the dearest being in all his creation. (see Figure. 9.3) God's love for Mary *is* creation's joy. This idea is not a theological fancy. Indeed, it is expressed constantly in the Byzantine liturgy, *'In you all creation rejoices'* and is portrayed in its iconography.

But St Romanos and the Hymn are at one in seeing Mary as the mighty intercessor for all of mankind before the face of God. In both the theme of her universal motherhood reaches its greatest height. Speaking to Christ, the Virgin affirms it.

"I am not simply your Mother...but for all men I beseech you. You have made me the mouth and the glory of my whole race. In me your world has a mighty protectress, a wall and a support. The exiles from the paradise of delights look to me." [167]

---

[167] Romanos, "On the Nativity of the Virgin Mary", I,474ff, in J.B. Pitra, *Analecta Sacra*, I (1876), 11.

Figure 9.3
Joy of all Creation

Let there be no mistake. The high Marian statements of the Akathistos Hymn and St Romanos are always counterweighted with the fact that whatever the glories of Mary, they are the work of her Son and come about by his power. But with a kind of heavenly delicacy, it is never Christ who reminds his Mother of her creatureliness. In all this sacred poetry it is Mary who does this. She reminds us that *'he who is mighty has done great things for me, and holy is his name'*

This God-ordained role of protectress of all the human race (also an ecclesiological statement, in that Mary and Church symbolise each other) is a convenient place to consider a particular feast, unique to our Churches in the East. If dire events had not dictated the development of the feast of the Protection (Intercession) of the Mother of God, the sheer weight and direction of the Church's theology of Mary would have finally given it its own separate liturgical festival amongst the other great Marian feasts. The Russians call it *'Pokrov' and* it was the Church of ancient Rus that chose to develop it, perhaps because certain aspects of the theology of the feast, known but little celebrated amongst the Greeks, spoke particularly to the Slavic Christian experience of following Christ.

The Protecting Veil, *'Pokrov.'*

The literary source of the feast of the Veil/Protection of the Mother of God on 1 October is the Greek *Life of St Andrew the Fool* which was translated quite early into Slavonic and was very popular with the Slavs. Although the story is about the saving of Constantinople, as is the icon (of which there are only Slav examples, as far as I know), the Slavs took it to themselves and made 1 October the feast. It is now in the Greek Synaxarion, but later, on 28 October. [168]

The story of St Andrew the Fool's vision is in the original Greek version of the *Life*, lines 3722-58, in Rydén's edition [169] This section tells of St Andrew's vision in the Blachernae church where the Mother of God appeared with her veil spread over the congregation and praying for the city of Constantinople.[170] (see Figure. 9.4) In all versions of this icon Andrew appears usually on the bottom right. He is a wild looking figure in tattered clothes and he is pointing to the holy vision and talking to a courtier, Epiphanios, who is some kind of patron. The vision occurred at the fourth hour of the night and they saw the Mother of God appearing

Figure 9.4
Intercession Protecting Vale

'very tall, from the Royal Doors, escorted by an awe-inspiring retinue in which there were, amongst others, the honourable Forerunner and the son of Thunder, holding her by the hand on both sides. (The icons do not show this holding of hands. Our lady stands separately)...Before their eyes she knelt and prayed for a long while, besprinkling with tears her godlike and immaculate face. Having finished her prayer she went into the sanctuary and prayed there for the people

---

[168] Icon of the Protection/Intercession of the Mother of God, Northern Province of Nvgorod, second half of the 16th century.

[169] *Life of St Andrew the Fool*, ed. Lennart Rydén, 2 vols., *Studia Byzantina Upsaliensia*, 4, (Uppsala: Uppsala University Press, 1995), 254.

[170] The girdle and veil of the Virgin were prized relics kept in this same Church from the time of the Emperor Leo I in the 5th century. The feast day of their translation to Blachernae, 2 July, is the origin of the much later Western feast of the 'Visitation'.

standing around. As she prayed she removed with beautiful dignity her veil that she had on her immaculate head, appearing like a flash of lightning and spread it (it was large and awe-inspiring) with her immaculate hands over all the people that were standing there. For a long time the admirable men saw it stretched out over the congregation, radiating the glory of God like an electrum. As long as the most Holy Mother of God was there the veil was also visible...but her favour she left to those who were there.'

The dates for this appearance vary wildly from the 8th to the 10th century, but in this vivid story, as in no other, we can come to understand something of the inner spiritual climate of the strongly increased devotion to Mary that occurred between the 5th and the 8th century. In this developing Marian tradition of the early empire, Mary is a mediator who answered the prayers of the faithful who called upon her, full of compassion for mankind. Mary Cunningham has noted that the fact that she prays is revealing in itself;

> the power to save comes not from herself but from God, with whom she stands in a unique relationship. The text also suggests the Virgin's accessibility to ordinary men and women. She is ready to answer every prayer and to help in any difficulty.[171]

Following Cunningham we should note that Mary appears *within* the Church and as part of the Church. However, in the discussion of whether it was her virginity or her maternity that commended her to the Church, Cunningham correctly notes that

> her virginity and her maternity are in no way ambiguous. They are rather described by the fathers as essential paradoxes which stem directly from the greatest paradox of all, the Incarnation of Christ.[172]

However, it is her motherhood which is to the fore in this icon. While her virginity is important theologically as guaranteeing the divine identity of her Son, in the realm of prayer and intercession it is her motherhood that is paramount. As far as I know, no commentator has given attention to the veil itself as it is portrayed in the icon. We should note that it is always red. Indeed, I propose that it recalls the veil that Mary was weaving from the scarlet and true purple in the *Protevangelium*. But as discussed earlier, she herself is the new veil of the temple of God. It is through her that the Holy One comes into the world, and that is nothing less than her divine motherhood itself. This is what the veil symbolises. But there is more. Commentators have neglected the ancient Graeco-Roman meaning of the veil. It is the sign of a married woman. In this case, a married woman who is bride and mother. Mary protects with her divine motherhood, while this icon also allows

---

[171] Mary Cunningham, "The Mother of God in Early Byzantine Homilies", *Sobornost* 10.2 (1988): 62-64.
[172] Cunningham, "The Mother of God", 62-64.

us to see that Mary, as Mother of God, is also figurative mother of mankind. She represents the link between the divine and human spheres and is thus intimately involved in our redemption and salvation.

The Eastern tradition has even more to say about the mystery of Mary's motherhood in terms of the spiritual life of each believer. Her protecting motherhood operates not only at the macrocosmic level of Church and society, but at the microcosmic level of the individual Christian. She is also the mother of the spiritual life in the believer. One example of this application from the Church's preaching will have to suffice. In a homily delivered on the feast of the Protection of Our Lady in 1884, Archbishop Dimitri Muretov took the theme of 'Rejoice, our Joy.' The sermon was republished in the *Journal of the Moscow Patriarchate* to celebrate the feast one hundred years later in 1984. The Archbishop says that she is both the '*Joy of the whole world*' and '*principally the Joy of Christians.*' He makes it clear that this is a role Mary plays empowered by her Son, and a relationship that is engendered at holy Baptism. Not only does the Christian die and rise with Christ in a renewal of their entire being, but they also enter into the relationship of the Redeemer and his Mother.

> She is their mother by grace of rebirth; their protection and
> guardian from all evil by the glory, power and might granted
> Her; the Giver of all good things, spiritual and physical, through
> Her maternal goodness, love and mercy to all believers in the
> Name of Her Son and God.[173]

The bishop speaks of a particular 'spiritual joy' and how to find one's way to it. He declares that the source of this spiritual joy, which alone can '*effectively comfort us in any sorrow*' is the '*All-Holy and Life-Giving Spirit-the Comforter.*' The Christian must win and preserve in themselves the grace of the All-Holy Spirit

> and be united in one spirit with the Lord Jesus Christ through
> faith, love and hope, prayer, repentance and communion in his
> Body and blood; by fulfilling His commandments and living a
> pious life in the fear of God.[174]

However, "*the Giver of this pure and holy joy in the Lord is the Most Holy Mother of God*". Known or unknown, Mary plays a role in the coming of grace to all souls.

> She, as the life-receiving and life-bearing source, is the first Receiver of
> the grace proceeding from God's Throne and the first giver of this grace to all
> believers who pray and ask.[175]

---

[173] Dimitri Muretov, "Homily", *Journal of the Moscow Patriarchate*, 14 (1984): 28-29.
[174] Muretov, "Homily", 28-29.
[175] Muretov, "Homily", 28-29.

Figure 9.5
Wisdom has Built Herself a House

This mystery is expressed liturgically and represented in the icon 'Wisdom has Built Herself a House' (see Figure 9.5) Christ, the Divine Word, as the Lord of the Banquet, seated to the lower left in a circle of eternity, is matched by Mary, her Divine Child in her lap presiding over the banquet of Wisdom. She is acclaimed by St Cyril with his scroll (lower right) and hailed and blessed by the kingly prophet from an ambo-like structure (middle). In the domed halls above the seven ecumenical councils dispense the word of Christ's truth historically. [176] However, *'the Giver of this pure and holy joy in the Lord is the Most Holy Mother of God.'* The eastern approach has reached its apogee in this remark, and I repeat this point, which is that known or unknown, Mary plays a role in the coming of grace to all souls.

The Entry of the Most Holy Theotokos into the Temple (21 November)

O Door of the Lord, to you I open
the doors of the Temple.
Enter with joy, for I know and believe
that the salvation of Israel will come now,
and from you will be born
the Word of God,
who grants great mercy to the Lord. [177]

---

[176] Novgorod Icon, mid 16th century.
[177] Raya and De Vinck, *Byzantine Daily Worship*, 518.

The feast of the Entry of the Theotokos in the Temple, celebrated on November 21, commemorates Mary's entrance into the Temple in Jerusalem as a young child. Mary remained in the Temple, living in the service of the Lord until the time came for her to be betrothed in marriage to Joseph.[178]

The feast originated in the East in the sixth century in Jerusalem, at the Church built in the Temple area by the Emperor Justinian. It was dedicated to Mary on 12 November 543 CE.[179] The early church Fathers, such as Germanus, Patriarch of Constantinople (patriarch 715-730 CE) and John Damascene, often preached on this feast and spoke of Mary as the special flower that was planted in God's House and nourished by the Spirit in preparation for the reception of God into her body and soul. It was not until the mid-twelfth century, however, that the feast day itself appeared in the orthodox liturgical calendar.[180] The feast was first celebrated in the West when Pope Gregory XI introduced it at Avignon in France in 1374.[181] In 1472, the celebration of the feast was extended to the universal church by Pope Sixtus IV,[182] and its universal observance throughout the West was introduced by Pope Sixtus V in 1585.[183]

Tradition tells us that when Mary was three years old, her parents, Anne and Joachim, decided that it was time to fulfil their promise to offer Mary to the Lord. Joachim invited some of the young virgins of the neighbourhood to accompany them to the Temple. He made the young virgins go in front of Mary, carrying burning lamps, so that the light from the lamps would capture Mary's attention on the way to her new home. In so doing, instead of looking back in sadness to her parents, from whom she must soon part, Mary's heart would be filled with gladness on her way to the temple.[184] Zacharias the High Priest, who was waiting for Mary at the gate of the Temple, blessed her saying: "The Lord God has magnified your name to all generations. And to the very end of time, the Lord by you will show his redemption to the children of Israel."[185] Zacharias then took Mary into the Holy of Holies,[186] placed her on the third step of the altar, and the Lord's grace descended upon her. Mary arose and "danced with her feet, and all the house of Israel loved her."[187] Mary served in the Temple, where she was miraculously fed by an angel,

[178] J.Matusiak, "Entrance of the Mother of God into the Temple" http://www.oca.org/pages/orth_chri/Q-and-A_OLD/Entrance-into-the-Temple.html. [accessed 24 October 2004], 1.

[179] The Church building did not last a century as it was destroyed by the Persians. See M. Mauriello, "November 21: Presentation of Mary" http://www.udayton.edu/mary/meditations/Nov21.html. [accessed 5 October 2004] , 1.

[180] Onasch and Schnieper, *Icons*, 149.

[181] Ouspensky and Lossky, *The Meaning of Icons*, 153.

[182] Mauriello, "November 21", 2.

[183] Matusiak, "Entrance of the Mother of God", 1.

[184] Mary and Ware, *The Festal Menaion*, 51. See also *The Protevangelion*, 3; "Feast of the Entrance into the Temple of Our Most Holy Lady the Theotokos" http://www.goarch.org/en/special/listen_learn_share/vmpresentation/learn/ [accessed 21 October, 2004] , 2.

[185] *The Protevangelion*, 3.

[186] The High Priest was the only one allowed to enter into the Holy of Holies. This happened once a year on the Day of Atonement. See, "Feast of the Entrance", 2.

[187] "Feast of the Entrance", 2. See also, *The Protevangelion*, 3.

until she was twelve years old. Having prayed to the Lord, Zacharias then betrothed Mary to Joseph, one of the widowers of the people.[188]

In the Russian icon for this feast (see Figure 9.6), Zacharias the High Priest, dressed in his priestly clothes, is standing on the step before the doors of the Temple. Joachim and Anne, both with halos, and the young virgins accompany the small child Mary to the steps where Zacharias stands. With her hands outstretched Mary reaches up to Zacharias who bends down to receive them. It is Zacharias who will guide Mary to the Holy of Holies.[189] On some icons Joachim and Anne are seen offering Mary to God and God's divine service with their arms outstretched. Above to the right, the childlike Mary is seated on a step of the Temple's Holy of Holies receiving nourishment from the Archangel Gabriel, who is depicted flying to the scene.[190] Despite Mary's small size, which indicates her young age, Mary is already the Mother of God, clothed in the maphorion which is also seen, for example, in icons of the Annunciation. Other Temple buildings are seen in the background.[191]

Figure 9.6
The Entry of the Theotokos in the Temple

---

[188] Mary and Ware, *The Festal Menaion*, 51. See also, *The Protevangelion*, 3.
[189] Onasch and A. Schneiper, *Icons*, 149.
[190] "Images of the Theotokos in Byzantine Iconography" http://www.msu.edu/~rabbatjo/entrancetemple.htm [accessed 24 October, 2004], 2.
[191] Ouspensky and Lossky, *The Meaning of Icons*, 156.

The inner meaning of the feast of Mary's Entry into the Temple and of her dwelling there signifies Mary's "total dedication to God, in readiness for her future vocation as the Mother of the Incarnate God."[192] Mary is fed by the angel "because she is to become the Mother of Christ who grants great mercy to us all."[193] The main theme of the feast is the indwelling grace of the Holy Spirit that was present and active within Mary from the earliest moments of her life.[194] This theme is expressed in the Lamp-Lighting prayers of Vespers for the Feast: "All the heavenly powers were amazed at the sight of the Holy Spirit dwelling in you."[195]

The feast, like that of Mary's Nativity, is a feast that anticipates the kindness of God and the announcement of the good news of the salvation of humankind. In the words of the Troporian of the feast we hear that:

> Today is the prelude to God's munificence, and the announcement of the salvation to men: in the Temple of God the virgin is seen openly, foretelling to all the coming of Christ. Wherefore let us cry out to her with all our strength: 'Joy to you, Fulfillment of the Creator's Plan!' [196]

As Mary is honored the Church looks forward always to the Incarnation of the Son of God.[197]

The Nativity of Christ (25 December)

> *Today the Virgin gives birth to the Creator;*
>
> *Eden offers a cave;*
>
> *a star proclaims Christ the Sun to those who are in darkness;*
>
> *the Magi, enlightened by faith, adore Him and offer gifts to Him;*
>
> *the shepherds witness the marvel,*
>
> *and the angels glorify Him saying: "Glory to God in the highest,*
>
> *on earth peace, and good will towards all."[198]*

The feast of the Nativity of Christ was instituted in the fourth Century, shortly after the Council of Nicea in 325 CE when the Nicean Creed was formulated.[199]

The sources for the iconography of the feast are from the descriptions of Jesus' birth in the Gospels of Mark and Matthew, as well as James' apocryphal gospel (c.150

---

[192] Mary and Ware, *The Festal Menaion*, 51-52.
[193] Raya and De Vinck, *Byzantine Daily Worship*, 519.
[194] Mary and Ware, *The Festal Menaion*, 52.
[195] Raya and De Vinck, *Byzantine Daily Worship*, 517.
[196] Raya and De Vinck, *Byzantine Daily Worship*, 516.
[197] Mary and Ware, *The Festal Menaion*, 52.
[198] Raya and De Vinck, *Byzantine Daily Worship*, 563. See also, Evdokimov *Light From The East*, 22.
[199] Evdokimov, *Light From The East*, 19.

CE). It has its prototype on fifth and sixth century ampullae, in which pilgrims used to bring home oil from lamps burning in special places in the Holy Land.[200] Every element in the icon has symbolic meaning. The icon discloses the essence of the great event – the Incarnation of the Son of God – and shows the effect and consequences of that event on the world.[201] All creation takes part in the great event, and around the Christ Child each gives thanks in their own way:

> O Christ, what shall we offer You
>
> for your coming on earth as a Man for our sake?
>
> Every creature that has its being gives thanks to You:
>
> the angels offer theheavens give a star;
>
> wise men present their gifts
>
> provides a cave and the desert a manger.
>
> As for us, we offer You a Mother,
>
> A Virgin Mother.
>
> O God who are from all eternity,
>
> have mercy on us.[202]

Lamp-Lighting Psalms of Vespers for the Nativity.

"To this the icon adds gifts from the animal and vegetable worlds".[203] The setting of the scene is in a rock formation (see Figure 9.7). In the icon's centre one sees a cave of blackness, an empty space, which represents both the world, stricken with sin, and Sheol, the underworld where the dead were thought to dwell. In this darkness, but somehow in its foreground, one can see the Christ Child, who is always shown in swaddling clothes, foreshadowing his death and the burial clothing in which he was buried.[204] The child is lying in a manger that is depicted as a sepulchre in inverse perspective. An ox and an ass are peering over one side of the manger, drawing attention to the prophecy of Isaiah (Isa 1:3):

> The ox knows its owner,
>
> and the donkey its master's crib;
>
> but Israel does not know Me,
>
> my people do not understand Me.

By recalling this verse we are called to the knowledge and understanding of the Mystery of the Divine Dispensation.[205]

---

[200] Ouspensky and Lossky, *The Meaning of Icons*, 157.

[201] Ouspensky and Lossky, *The Meaning of Icons*, 157.

[202] Raya and De Vinck, *Byzantine Daily Worship*, 560-561.

[203] Ouspensky and Lossky, *The Meaning of Icons*, 157.

[204] Ouspensky and Lossky, *The Meaning Of Icons*, 157.

[205] Ouspensky and Lossky, *The Meaning of Icons*, 159.

Figure 9.7
The Nativity of Christ

The Mother of God is singled out from all the other figures in the icon by her central position and often by the size she is given. She is often portrayed as the largest person in the icon, even though others are in reality 'closer' to the viewer.[206] One always must remember that icons are not realistic representations of an event or a person, but vehicles by which the faithful are taught mysterious truth. The use of hierarchical perspective (the most important person having the central position and being exaggeratedly big) and inverse perspective (the diverging lines meeting in front of the picture, and not in a depth-creating vanishing point in the picture itself) are formal techniques to underline theological content. The Mother of God is shown as either reclining on a bed of red material, of a kind such as the Jews carried with them on their travels, or she is shown as kneeling, in a prayer-like position, on a light coloured material. She is either looking at her Son or away from him, more often than not, in the direction of Joseph. Mary is always painted in such a way which points to the absence of the usual suffering attached to childbirth. Around this central group of Mother and Child are grouped all the details which testify to the Incarnation and its effect on the whole world.

> As shepherds were spending the night playing their flutes, angelic powers suddenly appeared to them and proclaimed: Leave your campsite and your flocks. In song cry out with joy, for today is born Christ the Lord, who was pleased as God to save humankind.[207]

---

[206] Ouspensky and Lossky, *The Meaning Of Icons*, 159.

[207] Evdokimov, *Light from the East*, 20.

On the top part of the icon are two groups of winged angels, one on each side of the rock formation. On one side the angels are looking heavenwards, singing (and maybe clapping) songs of praise of God. On the other side, the angels are telling the shepherds of the Good News. The shepherds may be interpreted as representatives of the Jewish people, simple unsophisticated folk with whom the world on high enters into communication directly amid their everyday working life. On the other side of the rock formation are the wise men, men of learning, who have to accomplish a long journey from the knowledge of what is relative to the knowledge of what is absolute, through the object that they study.[208] They are represented as following a star and bearing their gifts for the newborn Child. Some iconographers have the wise men riding on horses, but all of them depict the wise men as being of different ages, which emphasises the fact that revelation is given independently of years and worldly experience.

> He who comes forth before the dawn from his Father without a
> mother today comes forth from you, O Mary, without a father,
> and a star reveals the news to men of learning, as the shepherds
> join in praising your ineffable childbearing, O full of grace.[209]

A threefold ray of light streams directly to the darkness of the cave from a circle in the sky. This circle in the centre high point represents God the Father who cannot be directly represented iconographically. This light indicates the involvement of the whole Trinity in the event of the incarnation and gives the icon the character of an epiphany.

> The ray connects the star with a part of a sphere that generally
> goes beyond the limits of the icon. In this way, the icon shows
> that the star is not only a cosmic phenomenon, but also a
> messenger from the world on high, bringing tidings of the birth
> of "the heavenly One upon earth." In the shepherds, the first
> sons of Israel to worship the Christ Child, the Church sees the
> beginning of the Jewish Church, and in the wise men – "the
> beginning of nations" – the Church of the Gentiles.[210] In the
> adoration of the wise men, the Church testifies that it accepts
> and sanctifies all human science leading towards it, provided
> that the relative light of the extra-Christian revelation brings
> those who serve it to the worship of the absolute light. [211]

By descending downwards into matter, into creation, God allowed himself to be 'woven in the depths of the earth' (Ps 139:15). The expression 'depths of the earth'

[208] Ouspensky and Lossky, *The Meaning of Icons*, 159.
[209] Evdikomov, *Light from the East*, 22.
[210] Ouspensky and Lossky, *The Meaning of Icons*, 159.
[211] Ouspensky and Lossky, *The Meaning of Icons*, 159.

refers here to the womb. Mary's womb is like a cave in which God dwells. Mary is the new Eve who brings God into the world, and by virtue of giving birth to God, the Theotokos links humanity to the creator in a new way.

Another detail emphasises that in the Nativity of Christ "the order of nature is vanquished" – the figure of Joseph.[212] He is not part of the central group because he is not the father of the Child; he is emphatically removed from that group.[213] Before him, under the guise of an old and bent shepherd stands the devil, tempting Joseph to doubt the miraculous Mystery taking place. In some icons, this satanic character is portrayed as the god Pan, clad in goatskins, unsuccessfully suggesting to Joseph that a birth contrary to the laws of nature is impossible. Joseph's posture tells us that he is deep in thought.

On the other side of the icon, at the bottom, one can see women bathing the Christ Child. The woman holding the Child is sometimes shown to be testing the temperature of the water being poured into the bath by another midwife. In some icons the bath is painted to suggest a chalice. This scene from everyday life shows clearly that the Child is like any other newborn babe, and is subject to the natural requirements of human nature.

Often a tree, a reference to the Cross of Jesus, separates this scene and the one opposite it. The icon thus teaches that Christ's birth, his suffering, his death and his resurrection are all part of God's plan of salvation.

The Theophany or Baptism of the Lord (6 January).

> *In those days Jesus came from Nazareth of Galilee and was baptized by John in the Jordan. And just as he was coming up out of the water, he saw the heavens torn apart and the Spirit descending like a dove on him. And a voice came from heaven, 'You are my Son, the Beloved, with you I am well pleased' (Mk 1: 9-11).*

The Baptism of the Lord is mentioned in all three synoptic gospels[214] and is alluded to in the Gospel of John.[215] It marks the beginning of Christ's public ministry and the first public proclamation of His divinity. This significant event has always been a major feast in the Eastern Church. Its origins are thought to have a connection to the pagan, and later Christian, blessings of the River Nile during its periodic flooding.[216] It is known as the Theophany, and celebrated on the sixth of January. The corresponding feast in the Western Church, the Epiphany, celebrates the arrival of the magi as the first showing of the infant Jesus to the non-Jewish world, although

---

[212] Ouspensky and Lossky, *The Meaning of Icons*, 159.
[213] Ouspensky and Lossky, *TheMeaning of Icons*, 160.
[214] Mark 1:9-11, Matt 3:13-17 and Luke 3:21-22.
[215] John 1:29-34.
[216] Onasch and Schnieper, *Icons*, 107.

the prayers of the feast always contained references to both Christ's baptism and the marriage feast at Cana. It was not until the reforms of Vatican II that the Baptism of the Lord was celebrated as a separate feast in the Western Church.[217] It is unusual that so great a difference about the importance of a particular feast should exist between the Eastern and Western Churches.

Why the ambivalence of the Western Church to what was obviously a major event in the life and mission of Christ? The answer probably lies in the theology of St. Augustine, which gave the emphasis in baptism to the release from sin and guilt. Allowing for an appreciation of the sacramental action of the Spirit, this follows to some degree the understanding of John the Baptist himself.

> Then Jesus came from Galilee to John at the Jordan, to be baptized by him. John would have prevented him, saying, 'I need to be baptized by you and do you come to me?'[218]

Why then did Christ, who was sinless, need to be baptized? Sharing something of his view of baptism, Western Christians shared the same puzzled attitude of John.[219] This makes the feast more of a mystery than a celebration.

> The waters saw Thee and were afraid; the Forerunner was seized with trembling and cried aloud, saying: 'How shall the lamp illuminate the Light? How shall the servant set his hand upon the Master?[220]

The icon shows a different understanding. The icon (see Figure 9.8) shows the baptism of Christ not to be about sin, but rather about the definitive entry of God into the fabric of the world. Here the presence of Christ makes sacred the world of nature, particularly the substance of water,[221] and the nature of the world is changed. The icon is also about the showing forth of the Trinity:[222] the Son in the waters of baptism, the Spirit descending in the form of a dove, and the Father speaking - since the barrier between Heaven and Earth is now demolished. The icon thus leads to a different understanding of baptism. If the baptism of Christ is about the entry of the living God into our broken and sinful world, then our baptism is about our entry, sinners that we are, into the life of God.

> At your Baptism in the Jordan River, O Christ, the worship due to the Holy Trinity was made manifest, for the voice of the Father bore You witness by calling You 'Beloved Son', and the

---

[217] G. Collins, *The Glenstal Book of Icons: Praying with the Glenstal Icons* (Dublin: Columba Press, 2002), 61.

[218] Matt 3:13-14.

[219] Collins, *The Glenstal Book of Icons*, 61.

[220] Mary and Ware , *The Festal Menaion* , 317.

[221] Forest, *Praying with Icons*, 67.

[222] Ouspensky and Lossky, *The Meaning of Icons*, 164.

Holy Spirit, in the form of a Dove, confirmed the immutability of this declaration. O Christ God who came forth and filled the world with light, glory to You![223]

Figure 9.8
The Baptism of the Lord

The centre of the icon is Christ. His divinity is shown by the angels who are there to attend him. Normally he is naked or only partially clothed, showing that he has stripped off his divinity and humbled himself to become man. This foreshadows another time when he will be stripped of his dignity on the cross. He stands in the flowing water, which is thus made sacred by his presence. The old order has been changed forever. This is shown by the small figure of the pagan river god who is either fleeing from Jesus or turning to worship him but is clearly no longer king of this domain. The universal extent of this transformation is shown by the sea creatures – usually red fish – in the waters of the river, while the river itself is portrayed more as a narrow sea.

At the top of the icon, directly above Christ, there is a symbolic tear in the heavens and the background changes from gold to black – a symbol of the mystery and unknowableness of God. Since the Father cannot be represented, the eternal order of heaven is indicated by a semicircle or some other geometric form. Sometimes a hand is shown to indicate the Creator.

A ray extends from heaven directly over Christ, linking Christ and the Father. Midway along this ray there is a sphere containing a dove to represent the Spirit.

---

[223] Raya and De Vinck, *Byzantine Daily Worship*, 591.

This is the only icon to use the dove as a symbol for the Spirit, even though such a representation is common in western religious art. It is justified here because of the gospel reference, but frowned on in other cases because the Spirit is not a dove – the Sprit has no corporal form. This structure of a central linking axis shows the icon of the Baptism of the Lord to be primarily an icon of the Trinity, showing the linkage between Father, Son and Spirit.

To the left of Christ stands John the Baptist. He is shown unkempt and dressed in animal skins, as wild and harsh as the barren landscape of the Icon. He stands as the last of the prophets, representing the old Jewish covenant of the law. Indeed, there is a strong similarity between his representation and traditional icons of the Old Testament prophets, notably Elijah. It is important to note that he is not a passive or fleeing figure, like the old river god. He is actively baptizing Christ, showing that the new order is the fulfillment of the old covenant, not its contradiction. It is the last of the great Jewish prophets who presents Christ publicly to the world for the first time.

> You appeared to the world today, and Your light, O Lord, has
> left its mark upon us. With fuller understanding we sing to You:
> "You came, You were made manifest, the unapproachable light.
>
> Kontakion of the Epiphany

The Holy Meeting of Our Lord or the Presentation of Christ in the Temple (2 February)

> *Today the gate of heaven swings open, for the Word of the Father,
> who has no beginning, has had a beginning in time without any
> loss to his divinity: He is offered by a Virgin Mother as a child
> of forty days to the Temple of the Law. The elder Simeon has
> received him in his arms and the servant has cried out to his
> master: "Dismiss me, for my eyes have seen your salvation!" O
> Lord who came into the world to save mankind, glory to you!*[224]

In accordance with the Law of Moses, forty days after the birth of a male child, his parents were to present the baby in the Temple and offer a sacrifice, either a lamb or a pair of turtledoves or pigeons, for purification from "the issue of her blood." (Leviticus 12: 1-13) The presentation of a firstborn son also signified a redemption, or a "buying back," since all firstborn creatures, whether human or animal, were considered to belong to God. Mary and Joseph obeyed this precept of the Law. They brought Jesus to the Temple, where he was blessed by the aged Simeon, and recognised by the Prophetess Anna. It is this event that is celebrated on the feast of the Presentation of the Lord. The feast is also known

---

[224] Raya and De Vinck, *Byzantine Daily Worship*, 628

in the Christian East as the Meeting of the Lord, the Purification of the Virgin or simply as the Holy Meeting.[225]

> On Mount Sinai, Moses saw the back of God, and he heard God's voice as a storm raging in the darkness around him. This same God took flesh without change, and now Simeon has taken him into his arms. For the old man, life is now complete, and so he prepares joyfully to depart this life, saying: Now you may let your servant go in peace, Master, as you said you would.[226]

Scripturally the icon has three sources of inspiration: Exodus 13:2 speaks of the Consecration of the firstborn son to God; Leviticus 12:6-8 tells of the purification of the mother, forty days after the birth of a male child; Luke 2: 22-39 relates the event of Christ's presentation in the Temple and provides the source of the iconography. Celebrated on 2 February, the Feast is a celebration of the Holy Meeting, where the Old Testament and the New Testament unite.

The feast is of Palestinian origin.[227] The nun Egeria (or Aetheria), from the Roman province now known as Spain, saw it celebrated in Jerusalem at the end of the fourth century with a procession and great solemnity. It was introduced in Constantinople in the sixth century under Justin and Justinian. It made its way to Rome in the seventh century. The practice of holding lighted candles during the office of the Hypapante (Gk. "meeting") was introduced in Jerusalem in about 450 CE, and has been preserved in the West: hence the name of "Candlemas" ("Chandeleur" in France and "Lichtmesse" in German-speaking countries).[228]

The first known representations of the Presentation of Christ in the Temple are found in a mosaic in Santa Maria Maggiore from the fifth century, and on an enamelled cruciform reliquary now housed in the Lateran Museum from the end of the fifth or beginning of the sixth century.[229] The iconography of the Feast of the Hypapante was finally established during the ninth and tenth centuries.

> Rejoice, O full of grace, O Theotokos and maiden pure, for from you there arose the sun of justice, Christ our God, who enlightens those in darkness. You, too, exult and be glad, just and aged Simeon, for you bore in your arms the saviour and redeemer of our souls, and from him we all received the grace of resurrection.[230]

---

[225] Ouspensky and Lossky *The Meaning of Icons*, 168.
[226] Evdokimov *Light from the East*, 31.
[227] Ouspensky and Lossky, *The Meaning of Icons*, 168.
[228] Ouspensky and Lossky, *The Meaning of Icons*, 168.
[229] Ouspensky and Lossky, *The Meaning of Icons,* 169.
[230] Evdokimov, *Light from the East*, 31.

The scene of 'the meeting' takes place in its own space, seemingly in front of three buildings (see Figure 9.9). The buildings represent a Synagogue, the Temple and a Church, thus representing the 'meeting' of the Old Testament and the New Testament in the new Church of Christianity. The action of the 'meeting' takes place before an altar, which is depicted sometimes with a cross, sometimes with a book or scroll upon it. On one side of the altar is the Mother of God, and on the other side is Simeon.

Figure 9.9
The Presentation of Christ in the Temple

Sometimes, one sees the Christ child carried by his mother, or rather, she is handing him over to Simeon, but more often it is Simeon who is holding him in his arms. Christ is never shown in swaddling clothes, but is habitually clothed in a short tunic, which often leaves his legs bare. He is seated, rather majestically, on the outstretched arms of Simeon. His gaze is concentrated on the old Prophet. Sometimes he is seen giving a blessing.

The Mother of God is shown either passing her Son over to Simeon, or more usually having passed him over. Her tunic, usually green, under a crimson veil, always covers her hands. The Virgin's feet are always covered, usually by red slipper-type footwear. She is deeply moved by the words of Simeon:

> This child is destined for the falling and the rising of many in Israel, and to be a sign that will be opposed so that the inner thoughts of many will be revealed – and a sword will pierce your own soul too (Lk 2: 34-35).

The figure of Simeon is given great importance. A just and pious old man, he was "looking forward to the consolation of Israel."[231] God had assured him that he would not die before he had seen Christ the Saviour (Lk 2:26). The liturgical texts exalt him as the greatest of the prophets, even more than Moses. Simeon deserves the title of 'He who has seen God,' for to Moses God appeared enveloped in darkness, whereas Simeon carried the eternal Incarnate Word in his hands.[232] In one of the liturgical texts he is given the epithet "The God Receiver."[233] The aged prophet asks the Lord to allow him to announce the Incarnation:

> Master, now you are dismissing your servant in peace, according to your word: for my eyes have seen your salvation, which you have prepared in the presence of all peoples, a light for revelation to the Gentiles and for glory to your people Israel (Lk 2: 29-32).

There is nothing to indicate the priestly dignity of Simeon. His head is not covered, having the long hair of a Nazarene. His long green garment reaches down to his bare feet.[234] He is leaning forward in an attitude of welcoming the Christ child who is sitting nobly on his covered hands, another sign of veneration. In some icons, Simeon is portrayed on a podium to give him even greater importance.

The prophetess Anna, who had been serving God night and day in the Temple, is depicted as standing behind Simeon. Like Simeon, she had lived in expectation of the Messiah. She is standing in profile; her eyes are uplifted to express prophetic inspiration. More often than not, she is dressed in a green tunic with a red veil. She and Simeon represent the fullness of time, that peaceful fullness where men and women stand confidently in God's everlasting peace.[235]

Joseph is standing beside or behind Mary and is holding, as a gesture of offering, the two turtledoves to fulfil the Law of Moses. The two birds signify the Church of Israel and that of the Gentiles, as well as the two Testaments, of which Christ is the unique head.[236]

> The prophetess had taken to spending all her time in the temple in prayer, and the old man kept praying to be released from the bonds of this life. When finally he held in his arms the creator of all and found his release, the two old people rejoiced and prepared for eternal life.[237]

[231] Evdokimov, *Light from the East*, 28.
[232] Ouspensky and Lossky, *The Meaning of Icons*, 168-169.
[233] See the concluding prayers of the Proskomedia.
[234] See Ouspenky and Lossky, *The Meaning of Icons*, 169.
[235] Evdokimov, *Light from the East*, 28.
[236] Ouspensky and Lossky, *The Meaning of Icons*, 168.
[237] Evdokimov, *Light from the East*, 32.

The Annunciation (25 March)

The Archangel was sent to the pure Virgin
and with his greeting 'Hail!'
he brought good tidings,
that the Deliverer would come forth from her.
And so, accepting his salutation with faith,
she conceived Thee, the pre-eternal God,
who wast pleased to become man
ineffably for the salvation of our souls.[238]

Troparion of the Feast. Tone 4.

The feast of the Annunciation, celebrated on 25 March, commemorates both God's plan for the salvation of humankind in becoming the Son of the Virgin Mary, and the human response of Mary in freely accepting what God wanted of her in the accomplishment of His plan. Mary accepted the vocation offered to her by God, through the message of the Archangel Gabriel, to become the Mother of God, and as the God-bearer (Theotokos) she shares in God's redemptive mission. The religious service of the feast is filled with wonder at the great mystery of God's humility in becoming 'one of us,' and deep inner joy at the response of Mary's love and obedience which forms a crucial step in the accomplishment of our salvation.[239]

The feast of the Annunciation had its origins in the ancient Church. The early Christians used different titles such as the "Conception of Christ" and "Good Tidings of the Angel to Mary" for the naming of the feast. In the fourth century, Saint Athanasius the Great called it "the first in the line of feasts," as this feast celebrated the beginning of the salvation of humankind. The feast became significantly more celebrated during the Nestorian heresy of the fifth and sixth centuries, and received its current title, the Annunciation, in the seventh century. The feast of the Annunciation was introduced in Rome sometime between 660 CE and 680 CE and was celebrated as a solemnity of the Lord when Pope Sergius 1 (d. 701 CE), himself from the East, added the feast to the Roman calendar of the Church.[240]

The story of the Annunciation is told in St Luke's Gospel (Lk 1:26-38), and the tradition that tells of the work that Mary was actually doing at the time of the Angel's appearance. She was spinning scarlet and purple thread for making the new veil for the Temple in Jerusalem. This comes from the story of her life as told in

---

[238] Raya and Vinck, *Byzantine Daily Worship*, 756,

[239] Mary and Ware, *The Festal Menaion*, 60. See also, Baggley, *Doors of Perception*, 128.

[240] Other names for the feast were: "Good Tidings about Christ", "The Beginning of Redemption". See, A. Mileant, "The Feast of Annunciation: The Beginning of Our Salvation", trans. A. Perede http://www.fatheralexander.org/booklets/english/blagov_e.htm [accessed 15 November2004],1. See also, J. Kelly, "Heresy/Heretics", in *The Modern Catholic Encyclopedia*, Revised ed. (1994), 376. The Nestorians taught that the human Christ and the Divine Son of God were two separate persons. This teaching was condemned by the Council of Ephesus in 431 CE; Onasch and Schneiper, *Icons*, 150.

the apocryphal Protevangelium of St James. The iconography of the Annunciation, dates back to the second century where an image of the Annunciation exists in the catacomb of Priscilla in Rome.[241]

In the sixteenth century Russian icon of the Annunciation (see Figure 9.10), the Archangel Gabriel is depicted on the left hand side, with his feet wide apart, as if he is running to bring the Virgin Mary the good news that she will conceive without seed and bear a Son who is the pre-eternal God and Redeemer of all humankind.[242] The Archangel Gabriel holds a staff, the symbol of a messenger, in his left hand. As he delivers the message of good news to Mary, he extends his right hand forward towards her and looks above towards the source of his message. The colors in the icon and the posture of the Archangel Gabriel convey something of the wonder and joy that are linked with the feast. [243]

Figure 9.10
The Annunciation

Mary is depicted on the right side of the icon, sitting on seat with a platform under her feet. The seated position of Mary emphasizes the honor she has as the Mother of God. She is higher in honor than the Cherubim, and more glorious than the "Six-Winged and Many Eyed Seraphim."[244] In other icons, Mary is seen standing

---

[241] Ouspensky and Lossky, *The Meaning of Icons*, 172.

[242] Raya and Vinck, *Byzantine Daily Worship*, 660. See also, Mary and Ware, *The Festal Menaion*, 447. Mattins, Tone Four (Same Tone).

[243] Ouspensky and Lossky, *The Meaning of Icons*, 172. See also, Baggley, *Doors of Perception*, 128.

[244] "Feast of the Annunciation of Our Most Holy Lady, the Theotokos and Ever Virgin Mary" http://www.goarch.org/ en/special/listen_learn_share/annunciation/learn/index.asp?pri [accessed 15 November, 2004] . See also, Raya and

as if she is listening to a royal command. In this icon, as in most icons of the Annunciation, Mary holds a skein of scarlet thread in her left hand.[245]   Mary is performing the task given to her by Zachary the High Priest of spinning scarlet and purple thread to be used in the making of a new veil for the Temple.[246]

The icon captures the moment the Archangel Gabriel appears to Mary with his greeting. Mary turns and, in her surprise, she drops the spindle over her right shoulder. The expression of Mary's perplexity and surprise at the good news is shown in the gesture of Mary's right palm, which is held upwards and outwards. In this icon, the Archangel Gabriel and Mary do not look at each other. Their eyes are turned upwards towards the portion of a sphere, the symbol of the high heavens. The three rays coming from it depict the action of the Holy Spirit. The directions in which Mary and the Archangel Gabriel are looking converge in the three descending rays. This detail expresses the mutual consent between God and the Virgin Mary as spoken of in the service of the feast:

> An angel ministers at the wonder;
>
> a virgin womb receives the Son.
>
> The Holy Spirit is sent down;
>
> the Father on high gives His consent;
>
> and so the covenant is brought to pass
>
> by common counsel.[247]

The depiction of Mary's movement and the whole of her attention upwards signify that her consent is an active acceptance in which she surrenders her whole self to God's will. In some icons Mary is shown pressing her right palm to her breast in a gesture of acceptance, while her head is bowed in consent.[248]

The three star symbols on Mary's red cloak – or maphorion – signify Mary's virginity before, during and after the birth of Jesus. Mary is the ever-Virgin Mary. The red cloth draped between the buildings indicates that the event of the Annunciation took place indoors.[249]

The Incarnation was both the work of God and of the Virgin Mary. Out of God's loving kindness for humankind, God chose to become a human being and desired that the Virgin Mary would willingly agree to be the one from whom the Word would become 'flesh.' Mary's response, in which she said "yes", or "let it be done",

---

Vinck, *Byzantine Daily Worship*, 659. Sixth Tone at Vespers.

[245] In rare cases Mary is seen holding a scroll in her hands. See Ouspensky and Lossky, *The Meaning of Icons*, 172.

[246] "Feast of the Annunciation of Our Most Holy Lady", 3. See also, *The Protevangelion*, 4.

[247] Tone 4 of the Vigil Service Great Compline from Mary and Ware, *The Festal Menaion*, 445. See also, Ouspensky and Lossky, *The Meaning of Icons*, 172-173.

[248] Ouspensky and Lossky, *The Meaning of Icons*, 173.

[249] M. Ritchey, "The Icon of the Annunciation " http://www.melkite.org/Mediation3.html.[accessed 16 November, 2004], 2.

to becoming the Mother of God, was not a forgone conclusion. She was an active participant in God's plan of salvation history in that she freely accepted in faith the vocation offered to her by God to become the temple and dwelling place of the Incarnate Son of God. Mary's doubts, which are expressed with the utmost directness to the Archangel in the vespers of the feast are as follows:

> You come to me in human form: why then do you speak in words beyond human understanding, saying 'The Lord is with you,' and "The Lord will dwell in your womb'? Explain to me how I am to become a spacious vessel, a dwelling place of holiness for the One who is above the Cherubim. Mislead me not, for I know no pleasure of the body nor do I know man: how then shall I give birth to a Son?'

This text makes it quite clear that when Mary accepted the will of God she did so consciously and deliberately, in total freedom and in complete faith. Mary is honoured, not only because God chose her, but also because she herself made the right choice.[250] The Acathist Hymn celebrates the event of the Annunciation and sings Mary's praises:

> Hail, O Lady, unique gateway through whom the Lord has passed!
>
> Hail, O you who, through your maternity,
>
> have shattered the locks of Hades!
>
> Hail, divine access towards salvation for the saved,
>
> O you so perfectly worthy of our praise![251]

The Transfiguration (6 August)

> *How many times since our youth, Lord, have we begged for your mercy, only to go on taking it for granted! Unlike the prophet David, we have failed to attain repentance. During these days when we celebrate the Transfiguration of your Son, we implore you to bathe us in his light, that we may understand repentance and persevere in our pursuit of it. We beg you O God: With this feast, make us cleaner than spring water; wash us, and make us whiter than snow.*
>
> *By the grace and mercy and love for us of your only Son, with whom you are blest, together with your all-holy, good, and life-giving Spirit, now and forever, and unto ages of ages.[252]*

---

[250] Mary and Ware, *The Festal Menaion*, 60-61.

[251] Raya and Vinck, *Byzantine Daily Worship*, 961.

[252] Evdokimov, *Light from the East*, 61.

The origins of the feast of the Transfiguration are Scriptural. The narrative is related in the Synoptic Gospels and cited by one of the eyewitnesses in 2 Peter 1:16-18.

The feast of the Transfiguration is an ancient feast, although Aetheria – at the end of the fourth century – makes no mention of it. However, Nicephorus Callixtus[253] claims that St. Helen had built a church on Mt Tabor in 326.[254] Excavations seem to confirm this.[255] Homilies on the Transfiguration lead one to conclude that it was celebrated in the East well before the eighth century, when it appears as already a great solemnity, endowed with a canon by St. John Damascene.[256] In the West, it has been commemorated since antiquity on the second Sunday of Lent. Pope Clement recognised the feast as a second rank festival in 1475, whereas in the East it has been celebrated as a major feast since at least the seventh century.

In iconography, the symbolic images of the Transfiguration (such as in St. Apollinare in Classe in Ravenna, sixth century) were supplanted very early by direct representations of the evangelical event. The Gospel gives two accounts of the event. Mark and Matthew have the apostles falling after having heard the voice of the Father and seen the bright light. In the Lucan account, the apostles awake from a deep sleep to see the glory of the Christ. This latter version is found in the fresco of Toqale in Cappodocia (ninth-tenth century) where the apostles are represented as seated. St. John Chrysostom fused together the two versions in a commentary.[257]

The attitudes of the apostles vary in the different representations. (see Figure 9.11). Starting in the eleventh century, St. Peter (on the left) will always be represented as kneeling, with one hand either protecting himself from the dazzling light or raised in a gesture to accompany the words he addresses to Christ. St. John, always in the middle, is depicted as falling, with his back to the light. St. James is shown as falling, often on his back with one hand protecting himself from the brilliance of the light. Each of the apostles is shown as falling precipitately from the rugged summit, quite overwhelmed by the vision. This iconographic type became general in the fourteenth century at the time of the controversy over the Light of Tabor.[258] The discussion arose out of a disagreement concerning the nature of this light. The opponents of Palamas saw in the Taboric light a natural, created phenomenon. By contrast, for St. Gregory Palamas, the Taboric light "is the unchangeable beauty of the prototype, the glory of God, the glory of the Holy Spirit, a ray of divinity;" [259] that is, the energy of the divine nature which at the same time properly belongs

---

[253] Hist. Eccles., 1, VIII, c. 30; P.G. 146, col. 113 CD.
[254] Origen, Commentary on Ps. 1xxxviii, sec. 13; P.G. 12, col. 1548D.   See also, Ouspensky and Lossky, *The Meaning of Icons*, 211.
[255] Pere Barnabe d'Alsace. *Le Mont Thabor* (Paris, 1900), 58-61, 133-154.   See also, Ouspensky and Lossky, *The Meaning of Icons*, 211.
[256] St. John Damascene P.G. 96, coll. 848-852. See also, Ouspensky and Lossky, *The Meaning of Icons*, 211.
[257] St. John Chrysostom On Matthew, Homily 56; P.G. 58, coll, 552-553. See also, Ouspensky and Lossky, *The Meaning of Icons*, 211.
[258] Ouspensky and Lossky, *The Meaning of Icon*, 212.
[259] Details of the controversy of the Taboric Light can be found in Ouspensky *Theology of the Icon*, 238.

to the three persons of the Holy Trinity, an external manifestation of God. The intention was to underline in iconography the uncreated character of the Light of the Transfiguration. The eyes of the three apostles, sinners like ourselves, and accustomed as we are to the darkness of the world, were for a moment transformed so that they could see the "uncreated" light of the Spirit, the vision of the divine energies.

Figure 9.11
The Transfiguration

Both Moses and Elijah had a secret vision of God on other mountains. Moses face shone so brilliantly that the Hebrews were struck with fear (Exod 34:30). Elijah heard God speak to him in the still, small sound of a breeze (1 Kings 19:13) and was carried off in a chariot of fire. Elijah, on the left in this icon, is shown as an old man with long hair. Moses, on the right, is shown as holding the book of the law, the tables of the Decalogue. St. John Chrysostom[260] gives several reasons to explain their presence. Essentially they represent the law and the prophets.

Evdokimov points out that in sharp contrast to the figures at the bottom of the icon, Christ is standing straight and motionless. Serenity emanates from him as he converses with the two great men of Hebrew Scripture.[261] His clothing is gloriously bright. The geometrical hexagon behind the glorious Christ is inscribed within the circle of a mandorla, representing the "bright cloud" which reveals the transcendent source of the Divine energies. Three rays point downwards to the apostles, indicating that the action in the Transfiguration is Trinitarian. This symbolism is found in other icons, such as the Annunciation and the Theophany.

---

[260] St. John Chrysostom P.G. 58, col. 550-551.
[261] Evdokimov, *Light from the East*, 58.

> You were transfigured on the mount, O Christ God, revealing
> your glory to your disciples as they could bear it. Let your
> everlasting light shine upon us sinners. Through the prayers of
> the Theotokos, O Giver of Light, glory to you.
> (Troparion)

The Church Councils of the fourteenth century (1341, 1347 and 1351-1352) made the theme of the Transfiguration their special concern in formulating the understanding of grace as founded on the dogmatic distinction between the inaccessible essence and the communicable energy of God.[262]

> St. Gregory Palamas (died 1359), in defending the traditional
> teaching on the Lord's Transfiguration against the attacks of
> certain rationalist theologians, well understood how to give full
> value to the importance of this evangelical event for Christian
> spirituality and dogma.[263]

"God is called Light," he said, "not according to His essence, but according to His energy."[264] The Divine Light is neither material nor spiritual, for it transcends the order of the created; it is the "ineffable splendour of the one nature in three hypostases."[265] "The light of the Lord's Transfiguration had no beginning and no end; it remained uncircumscribed (in time and space) and imperceptible to the senses, although it was contemplated with bodily eyes ... but by a transmutation of their senses the disciples of the Lord passed from the flesh to the Spirit."[266]

> The first meaning of the Transfiguration then is the glorification
> of the Son by the Father before the final degradation. It is a
> glorious manifestation of the Trinity: the voice of the Father, the
> luminous cloud, and the Son, all three in an intimate unity. The
> Transfiguration affects every person, living or dead: 'On this
> day on Mount Tabor Christ has transformed Adam's darkened
> nature; having covered him with his glory he divinises him'
> (Vespers).[267]

There is an eschatological quality to the Icon of the Transfiguration. Christ appears as the Lord of the living and the dead, coming in the glory of the future age. The

---

[262] Ouspensky and Lossky, *The Meaning of Icons*, 209.

[263] Ouspensky and Lossky, *The Meaning of Icons*, 209.

[264] St. Gregory Palamas Against Akindynos (table of contents published in Migne) VI, 9 in P.G. 150, col. 823, Ouspensky and Lossky, 211.

[265] St. Gregory Palamas Homily 35; P.G. 151, col, 448D.

[266] St. Gregory Palamas Homily 34. P.G. 151. col. 429A. On the theology of the Transfiguration according to Gregory Palamas, see Basil Krivoshein, "The Ascetical and Theological Teaching of Gregory Palamas". *Eastern Churches Quarterly*, vol III, 1938, Ouspensky and Lossky, 212.

[267] Evdokimov, *Light from the East*, 59.

Transfiguration was "an anticipation of his glorious coming", says St. Basil,[268] the moment which opened a perspective of eternity in time.

> This is an icon of quite violent force, explosive quality; it shows an extreme experience. We may find it difficult to relate to at first for that reason: we may be struck and impressed by it, yet feel also that nothing in our experience corresponds to this. We weren't there, we haven't seen the skies opening, the light suffusing the lonely figure on the rock, the weight of divine presence forcing us back, bowing us down. But the point of this, as of any icon, is not either to depict or to produce some kind of special experience in that sense: it is to open our eyes to what is true about Jesus and the saints. And what is true about Jesus is – if we really encounter it in all its fullness – shocking, devastating: that this human life is sustained from the depth of God without interruption and without obstacle, that it translates into human terms what and who God the Son eternally is. The shock comes from realising this means that God's life is *compatible* with every bit of human life, including the inner terrors of Gethsemane (fear and doubting) and the outer terrors of Calvary (torment and death) … the point about this image of the Transfiguration is to reinforce how the truth about Christ interrupts and overthrows our assumptions about God and about humanity.[269]

The icon is an act of witness and a revelation of transfiguration. We were made in the image and the likeness of God, our Creator, but the image has been damaged and the likeness lost, as a result of our sin. Since Adam and Eve, only in Jesus Christ were these attributes fully intact. Thomas Merton once reflected on an icon of Christ:

> What one 'sees' in prayer before an icon is not an external representation of a historical person, but an interior presence in light, which is the glory of the transfigured Christ, the experience of which is transmitted in faith from generation to generation by those who have "seen," from the apostles on down … So when I say that my Christ is the Christ of icons, I mean that he is not reached through any scientific study but through direct faith and the mediation of the liturgy, art, worship, prayer, theology of light, etc., that is all bound up with the Russian and Greek tradition.[270]

---

[268] St. Basil Homily on Ps. Xliv, sec 5; P.G. 29, col. 400CD.

[269] Rowan Williams. *The Dwelling of Light: Praying With Icons of Christ* (Mulgrave, Vic.: John Garratt Publishing, 2003), 11-12.

[270] William H. Shannon, (Ed.) *The Hidden Ground of Love: The Letters of Thomas Merton on Religious Experience and Social Concerns* (New York: Farrar, Straus & Giroux1985), 637, 642-643.

The Dormition of the Theotokos (15 August)

Neither death nor tomb could hold the Mother of God.
She is always ready to intercede for us,
forever our steady hope and protection.
Since she is the Mother of Life,
Christ who dwelt in her ever-virginal womb lifted her up to life.[271]

The feast of the Dormition or the Falling Asleep of the Mother of God, the last major feast of the Byzantine liturgical calendar, commemorates the death, burial, resurrection and glorification of the Blessed Virgin Mary.[272] It marks the end of Mary's life on earth and celebrates her entry into heaven, where she already participates in the eternal and divine life of God. In the Orthodox East the feast of the Dormition places its focus on the death of Mary and the traditions associated with that event. In the Western Church this same feast, known as the feast of the Assumption, concentrates on Mary's bodily assumption rather than on her death.[273]

The apocryphal accounts of Mary's dormition (*Transitus Mariae*), while not strictly historical, provide evidence for a belief among the Christians of the fifth century that Mary, at her death, was assumed bodily into heaven.[274] The feast commemorating Mary's dormition became fixed as a liturgical feast in the East in the sixth century when the Emperor Maurice (582 CE – 602 CE) decreed that the feast be celebrated on 15 August throughout the Byzantine Empire. The incorporation of the feast into the Byzantine calendar led to more regular preaching on Mary's dormition and deeper insight into the meaning of the feast. Sermons such as those of St. John Damascene (d. c. 750 CE) show that the object of the feast included the glorification of Mary's soul and body, as well as her death. In the seventh century the feast of the Dormition of Mary was adopted in the West under Pope Sergius 1 (687 CE – 701 C E). From its beginnings in Rome the feast centred on the glorification of Mary's body rather than on her death. As a result, the title of the feast in the Western Church eventually changed from "Dormition" to "Assumption".[275] What began as

---

[271] Raya and Vinck, *Byzantine Daily Worship*, 756.

[272] Ouspensky and Lossky, *The Meaning of Icons*, 213. See also, D. Hickey, "Dormition of the Virgin", in *New Catholic Encyclopedia*, 2nd ed. (2003), 4: 875. The Christian belief in life after death and in the resurrection "when the body would be eternally reunited to the soul" led Christians to view "death not as the end of everything but as a transition into another life in which the body fell asleep and rested until awakened into eternal glory". As a result they commemorated the day of death, or "falling asleep", of the martyrs as their "birthday" into a new life.

[273] Baggley, *Doors of Perception*, 138.

[274] The writings of *Transitus Mariae*, a body of apocryphal literature, describe Mary's last hours in great detail. These writings, whilst highly imaginative and, on the whole, fictitious, satisfied the longing of Christians to know more about the passing of Mary since there was nothing about her death in the Sacred Scriptures. See Hickey, "Dormition", 875. See also, J. Langlinais, "Assumption of Mary", in *New Catholic Encyclopedia*, 2nd ed. (2003), 800.

[275] Hickey, "Dormition", 875-876. See also, J. Bur, *How to Understand the Virgin Mary* (New York: Continuum, 1996), 74. In 1950 Pius XII declared the Assumption of Mary to be dogma. While this truth was part of the universal faith of the Western and Eastern orthodox Christians, the Eastern Church, in contrast to the Roman Catholic Church, never declared Mary's assumption as dogma; Onasch and Schnieper, *Icons*, 152. The Eastern Orthodox belief is embodied in the feast of the Dormition of the Theotokos and is reflected in the icon painting of the feast.

a tribute to the anniversary of Mary's death became, in the West, a commemoration of the Assumption as such.[276]

The feast of the Dormition of Mary is based primarily on a tradition of the early Church concerning the death and assumption of the Blessed Virgin Mary. According to tradition Mary lived in the house of St. John the Evangelist in Jerusalem on Mount Zion, while the other apostles were preaching the Gospel in different parts of the then-known world. As Mary's death drew near, she expressed the desire to see the Twelve once more before she died. All of them except Thomas were miraculously carried on clouds to Jerusalem. St. Paul the Apostle and the bishops Dionysios the Areopagite, Hierotheos and Timothy were also said to be present with the Apostles at Mary's bedside. As Mary commended "her most pure soul into the hands of her Son" (Vespers, Tone 2), they saw Christ descend from heaven and receive his Mother's soul into his arms. Led by St. Peter, they proclaimed "things divine" and praised "Christ's astounding mystery" as they prepared Mary's holy body for burial, and carried "the Source of Life and the Temple of God" (Vespers, Tone 4) to a tomb especially prepared for her near Gethsemane. Athonios, a fanatical Jew who tried to interrupt the funeral procession by overturning Mary's bier, had both hands cut off by an angel with a sword. Sometime later his hands were miraculously restored.[277] Three days after the burial, Thomas arrived to have one final look upon the face of Mary, the Mother of God. When the apostles opened the tomb for Thomas, they found it empty. Mary then appeared to them and confirmed the fact of her bodily Assumption into heaven.[278] There is a firm kernel of truth concerning Mary's death and assumption, but the believer is not required to accept all teh setails of the story.

In the icon of the Dormition (see Figure 9.12) we see the Mother of God lying on her deathbed with her eyes closed and her hands crossed. Standing to the right and left of Mary's bed, with Peter and Paul in the foreground, are the grieving apostles and three bishops. Seized with dread, they all look at the "pure remains" of Mary with great sadness. Invisible in their midst, standing behind Mary's bier within a mandorla, is Christ in glory, accompanied by "the most sublime Powers of heaven" (Vespers, Tone 1). Christ has taken up the "all-luminous soul" of his Mother, which is represented as a small child wrapped in white swaddling clothes, and is ready to

---

[276] Langlinais, "Assumption of Mary", 800.

[277] In *The Apocryphal New Testament* (Being the Apocryphal Gospels, Acts, Epistles, and Apocalypses) translated by M. James (Oxford: Clarendon Press, 1955), the account in the Greek Narrative of the Discourse of St John the Divine of the Hebrew who touched Mary's bier reads as follows: "And behold as they bare her, a certain Hebrew named Jephonias, mighty of body, ran forth and set upon the bed, as the apostles bare it, and lo, an angel of the Lord with invisible power smote his two hands from off his shoulders with a sword of fire and left them hanging in the air about the bed. And when this miracle came to pass, all the people of the Jews that beheld it cried out: Verily he is the true God that was born of thee, Mary, mother of God, ever virgin. And Jephonias himself, being commanded by peter, that the wonderful works of God might be showed, stood up behind the bed and cried: Holy Mary that didst bear Christ which is God, have mercy on me. And Peter turned and said unto him: In the name of him that was born of her thine hands which were taken from thee shall cleave to their place. And immediately at the word of Peter the hands that did hang beside the bed of our lady went back and clave unto Jephonias: and he also believed and glorified Christ, even God, that was born of her". See page 208 verses 46-47.

[278] Raya and Vinck, *Byzantine Daily Worship*, 755. See also, Mary and Ware, *The Festal Menaion*, 63-64.

carry it to heaven.[279] She who once held her son in swaddling clothes is now held in her Son's arms.[280] Just as Mary gave her Son earthly life, her Son now helps his Mother to pass beyond this world into eternal and divine life: "You have been carried into life, you who are the Mother of Life."[281]

Figure 9.12
The Dormition

The six winged seraphim, the two cherubim and two angels in the mandorla glorify Mary's dormition. On some icons the multitude of angels present at Mary's Dormition forms a large outer border around a small mandorla which surrounds Christ. Some icons also picture the bodily assumption of Mary, showing her at the top of the icon within the mandorla of eternity and being carried by angels into heaven.

St. Peter incenses the bier and leads the prayers, and St. Paul is seen bowing low over Mary's feet. On some icons, St. John is seen bending his head near to the Virgin. Apart from the Apostles and the bishops, some versions of icons show groups of women, representing the faithful of Jerusalem, and Athonios the apocryphal Jew. On other icons, the Apostles are also depicted arriving on clouds from "every corner of the world" (Vespers, Tone 1). The lighted candle in front of Mary's bier symbolizes Mary as "'the Candelabra of Inaccessible Light.'"[282]

---

[279] Brentnall, "The Language of Orthodox Icons", 30-31. See also, Ouspensky and Lossky, *The Meaning of Icons*, 214; K. Parry, "Dormition", in *The Blackwell Dictionary of Eastern Christianity* , ed. Ken Parry et al. (Oxford, UK: Blackwell Publishers, 2000), 165.

[280] Forest, *Praying with Icons*,101.

[281] Evdokimov, *Light from the East*, 63.

[282] Brentnall, "The Language of Orthodox Icons", 30-31. See also, Ouspensky and Lossky, *The Meaning of Icons*, 214; Parry, "Dormition", 165; Baggley, *Doors of Perception*, 147.

The central teaching of this feast, according to the Orthodox tradition, is that Mary, like her Son, had undergone a physical death, was buried, and was raised from the dead on the third day. Mary's body could not experience corruption because it was the "Temple of the Lord" (Vespers, Tone 4). Her body, like that of her Son, was raised from the dead and Mary was taken up into heaven, in her body as well as in her soul, by her Son. Mary had passed beyond the general Resurrection of the Body, which all Christians await. She is already living in the age to come. Mary is the first human being to become deified, that is, to be made divine by grace, to participate in the eternal life of God through Jesus Christ the Incarnate Son of God. In Mary, we see our final destiny realized. From her place in heaven, Mary is intimately linked to all human beings and to the entire universe. She continues her care as mother to all of humanity. She is ever-watchful of each human being, and never stops interceding for them in her prayers. In Mary's intercession lies unfailing hope. "Let us, therefore, venerate her and beseech her, saying: ' O Lady, do not forget those who share your humanity and who celebrate your holy Dormition with fervor and love'" (Vespers, Tone 5).[283]

---

[283] Mary and Ware, *The Festal Menaion*, 65. See also, Ouspensky and Lossky, *The Meaning of Icons*, 213; Cross, *Eastern Christianity*, 36; Brentnall, "The Language of Orthodox Icons", 31.

CHAPTER TEN

MOVEABLE GREAT FEASTS OF THE LITURGICAL YEAR

The Entry of the Lord into Jerusalem (One week before Easter)

*People everywhere! All you nations! Everyone come forth! Behold
the king of heaven as he enters Jerusalem, the holy city, seated on
the colt of an ass as if on a lofty throne. Come behold him whom
Isaiah once saw; behold the bridegroom of the new Zion, for he
comes in the flesh to save us from our sins. And to celebrate his
pure and undefiled nuptials, the innocent children gather to sing
his praises, and so with them we also greet him, exclaiming: To
him who grants great mercy, Hosanna in the highest!* [284]

The sources or inspiration for the icon of the Entry of the Lord into Jerusalem are Scriptural, coming from both the Jewish and Christian writings. The Prophet Zechariah writes, "Rejoice greatly O daughter of Zion! Shout aloud, O daughter of Jerusalem! Lo, your king comes to you; triumphant and victorious is he, humble and riding on an ass, on a colt the foal of an ass".[285] Each of the four evangelists tells of Jesus' triumphal entry into Jerusalem and against this prophetic backdrop.[286]

Military commanders of the ancient world would make their triumphant entrance into a city riding on their warhorse. In this "Adventus" (Latin: 'the coming'), the proud commander would allow himself to be cheered by the people, and triumphant soldiers bearing weapons would be followed by prisoners and the spoils of war. Compared with such a display of power, the contrast to *The Entry Into Jerusalem* is striking. Jesus does not surround himself with armed guards but is attended by disciples who barely understand the intentions of the Divine Master. Such insights came later, at the Pentecost event. Jesus entered Jerusalem riding on a donkey.

> He who sits upon the throne of the cherubim, for our sake sits
> upon a foal; and coming to his voluntary Passion, today he hears
> the children cry "Hosanna!" while the crowd replies, "O Son of
> David, make haste to save those whom you have created.[287]

Icons depicting this event (see Figure 10.1) have a triumphal and festive quality which gives a foretaste of Easter Joy in the midst of Great Lent.[288] This festive character is portrayed through the brightly coloured cloaks spread out before the

---

[284] Evdokimov *Light From The East,* 41.
[285] Zech 9:9.
[286] Mt 21:1-11; Mk 11:1-11; Lk 19: 28-40 and Jn 12:12-19.
[287] Palm Sunday Matins, Tone 8.
[288] Ouspensky and Lossky, *The Meaning of Icons,* 176.

procession. The majestic Saviour is flanked by the apostles and townsfolk and rides upon the donkey as if seated on a throne. The donkey is depicted as a meek creature by its lowered head. It is perfect for a ruler with no army, no weapons, and no armour. Christ is the central figure in the icon; all the action takes place around him. The Saviour's head is usually turned to the apostles, but occasionally, Jesus is shown to be looking at the townsfolk. One hand is raised in a gesture of blessing, the other holds a scroll, a reference to the Pantocrator Christ Icon.

Figure 10.1
The Entry of the Lord into Jerusalem

The apostles and disciples (in some icons only two are portrayed, one being Saint Peter) are depicted deep in conversation, and their hand gestures indicate that their conversation is of great importance. Above them is shown a mountain often described as Golgotha by many commentators. Opposite the disciples the townsfolk are portrayed. Even though their eyes are turned to the Saviour, they are depicted as an unstable crowd who only a few days later will turn against the Christ. Above them one can see the city of Jerusalem, portrayed in either white or red. In between the city and the mountain opposite it, a tree is given prominence. This is a visual reminder that a tree will become the cross that Jesus will have to carry in a short while. Sometimes a child is depicted in the tree, sometimes cutting off a branch with an axe, or sometimes waving a palm that has just been chopped off.

The immediate cause of the welcome given to Jesus is the raising of Lazarus from the dead when "the great crowd that had come to the festival heard that

Jesus was coming to Jerusalem. So they took branches of palm trees and went out to meet him, shouting, 'Hosanna! Blessed is the one who comes in the name of the Lord – the King of Israel!'" (John 12:12-13). The palm branch, a symbol of joy and feasting, was used to welcome people of high rank.[289] As a symbol of valour, the palm of victory was presented to the conqueror. Here, one of the townsfolk is shown holding a palm branch, but it is the children in the icon who place their cloaks on the ground. Children play an important role in the icon of the Entry into Jerusalem.[290] Even though the evangelists do not specifically mention them, iconographers have on this occasion used their imagination to portray the crowd with children. It is reasonable to assume that children would have been part of the "great crowd" celebrating the feast and so, in the icon, children are portrayed as placing their cloaks on the ground, like rolling out the red carpet, or waving palm branches. One is reminded of the passage in 2 Kings, "Then hurriedly they all took their cloaks and spread them on the bare steps; and they blew the trumpet, and proclaimed, "Jehu is king" (2 Kings 9:13). Also, Christ's teaching is recalled: "Whoever does not receive the kingdom of God like a child shall not enter it" (Mk 10:15).

> According to the spiritual writer John Cassian (c.365-435) *The Entry into Jerusalem* may be interpreted on four different levels. The first, *literal* level refers to the historic event, namely that of Christ who rode in procession into the Jewish capital Jerusalem and was acclaimed as king by the crowd a few days before his crucifixion. On the *allegorical* or *typological* level Jerusalem stands for the Church that Christ established by his death and resurrection, and with which he unites himself through word and sacraments during every divine service. On the *moral* or *tropological* level, Jerusalem is the individual human soul that receives Christ in a spiritual way. On the last, *analogical* level Jerusalem refers to the eternal abodes in the world to come – the heavenly Jerusalem where the Kingdom of God will blossom in its fullness.[291]

St Epiphanius of Cyprus further explains the icon:

> Why did Christ, who previously walked everywhere, go up to Jerusalem riding on an animal? To show us that He would be raised up on the cross and glorified on it. What does the town represent? The disposition of the rebellious spirit of mankind evicted from Paradise, to whom Christ sent two disciples, namely, the two Testaments both Old and New. What does the donkey signify?

---

[289] Ouspensky and Lossky *The Meaning of Icons*, 176.
[290] Ouspensky and Lossky *The Meaning of Icons*, 177.
[291] Nes, *The Mystical Language of Icons*, 73.

> Without doubt, the synagogue that led its life beneath a burden and
> on the back of whose laws Christ would sit one day in triumph.
> What does the colt prefigure? The unbridled pagans whom no one
> could tame: neither the Law, nor fear, nor angel, nor prophet, nor the
> Scriptures, but only God, the *Word*. (quoted by Monk Gregory)[292]

The Eucharist is a prelude to the Church's entry into the Jerusalem that comes
from above. To underline this, the Byzantine liturgy sings the verse "Blessed is
he who comes in the name of the Lord" immediately before Holy Communion.[293]
The resonances of the Feast of the Entry into Jerusalem are also heard in the verse:

> Buried with you in Baptism, O Christ our God, we have been
> deemed worthy of immortal life thanks to your Resurrection,
> and we cry out this hymn of praise: Hosanna in the highest,
> blessed is he who comes in the name of the Lord.[294]

The Ascension (The Fortieth Day of Easter)

> *Jesus said to them ...when the Holy Spirit comes upon you,
> you will be filled with power and you will be witnesses to me
> in Jerusalem, in all of Judea and Samaria, and to the ends of
> the Earth." After saying this He was taken up to heaven as they
> watched Him and a cloud hid him from their sight. They still
> had their eyes fixed on the sky as He went away, when two
> men dressed in white suddenly stood beside then and said,
> 'Galileans, why are you standing there looking up at the sky?
> This same Jesus, who was taken from you into heaven, will
> come back in the same way that you saw him go to heaven'.
> Acts 1: 7-11.*

The fullest account of the ascension is that given in Acts (above), although it
is mentioned briefly in Luke[295] and very briefly mentioned in Mark.[296] Neither
Matthew nor John mentions the event. It is also important to note that in all three
scriptural texts, the fact of the ascension is given very little emphasis. The main
focus of each of the texts is on the commissioning of the church to continue Christ's
mission on Earth.

As a feast of the church, the ascension was originally celebrated together with the
resurrection on Easter Sunday. It was separated in the fourth century and combined
with Pentecost. It was not until the fifth century that it was fixed as the fortieth day

---

[292] Cited in Quenot, *The Icon*, 61.
[293] Evdokimov, *Light from the East*, 39.
[294] Evdokimov, *Light from the East*, 39.
[295] Luke 24: 50-53.
[296] Mark 16: 19-20.

of Easter and celebrated as a separate feast.[297] While there are some early ivories that have a different form, the current composition of the icon is very ancient. The Ampulla of Monza and the Rabula Gospels indicate that it dates from at least the fifth or sixth centuries:[298] the current form of the icon dates from about the same period as the celebration of the Ascension as a separate feast.

There are a number of interesting features about this icon (see Figure 10.2). The first is that, while the ascended Christ is prominent, He does not dominate. He shares the icon with Mary and the assembled apostles. Indeed, the figures of Mary and the apostles are drawn larger than that of Christ. This shows that the icon is not primarily concerned with the historical event of the ascension. Rather, it is concerned with the meaning of this event and with its significance for the church. This fact is reinforced by the presence of Mary and Paul in the icon. Mary is not mentioned as being present at the ascension in any of the accounts in Scripture, although it is possible that she was there and tradition certainly places her there, as is indicated by the text of the Divine Liturgy, such as the 9th canticle of the canon: "Rejoice, Thou Mother of Christ our God, seeing with the apostles Him whom thou didst engender ascending to heaven, and glorifying Him."[299]

Figure 10.2
The Ascension

[297] Onasch and Schnieper, *Icons,* 118.
[298] Ouspensky and Lossky, *The Meaning of Icons*, 199.
[299] Ouspensky and Lossky, *The Meaning of Icons*, 196.

While the presence of Mary is possible, but not mentioned in Scripture, the presence of Paul is historically impossible. The inclusion of Mary and Paul is meant to indicate the presence of the whole church. It is the whole church which is the witness to Christ's resurrection and ascension, and it is the whole church which is commissioned to now carry on His mission in the world. The icon thus shares the emphasis of the scriptural accounts.

Another interesting aspect of the icon is the centrality of the figure of Mary. She is shown between the two angels forming a central axis with the figure of the ascended Christ. She is shown elevated above the apostles, with a calm demeanor and with her hands raised in an all embracing gesture. If this icon is about the commissioning of the Church, Mary is shown to have a central significance as the personification of the Church. This follows an interpretation of the text of Revelation,[300] and the understanding of the early church about the central role of Mary, not just in the story of salvation, but in the mission of the Church. Just as Mary brought the incarnate Christ to the world, so the church would now bring the risen Christ to the world. Just as Mary was the mother of Jesus in his physical body, so she is still His mother in His mystical body - the church. It is worth noting also that at this time, before Pentecost, Mary was the spirit bearer for the church.

Mary is important in the icon for another reason also. This icon is about the completion of Christ's mission. Salvation has been won. It is now the work of the church to preach this good news and to realise on Earth the kingdom of God which has already been established. Just as Mary played a central role at the start of His earthly mission, his birth, so she plays a central role in its completion. The fine balance and symmetry of the icon also indicates completion, closure. One phase of God's action is finished and a new phase is about to start. Mary and the angels attend both the start and the finish.

This sense of completion is further enhanced by the figure of the ascended Christ. He is shown in a dark mandorla indicating that He has entered into the eternal mystery of God. This is reminiscent of the dark tear in the sky that is shown in the icon of Christ's baptism, the start of His earthly ministry. Then, the mystery of God's grace was flowing into creation through Christ. Now, Christ has returned to that mystery. In both cases he is attended by angels who show His divinity. In the icon of the Baptism of the Lord the central axis is formed between the three divine persons of the Trinity: the Father in heavenly mystery, the Spirit as a dove, and the Son immersed in the waters of the world. In the icon of the ascension, the central axis is formed by the ascended Christ in heavenly mystery and Mary as the centre of the Church. The icon shows that, just as God was present to the world through Christ in His incarnation, so Christ is present to the world in His church - as shown and presented by Mary and the gathered apostles.

---

[300] Rev 12:1-6.

> Thou hast ascended in glory O Christ our God, granting joy to
> Thy disciples by the promise of the Holy Spirit. Through the
> blessing they were assured that Thou art the Son of God, the
> Redeemer of the world! (*Troparion*).

In terms of geometry, the icon has one central, vertical axis of symmetry, which connects the ascended Christ and Mary, and it is divided into two halves horizontally, with Christ and His attendant angels in the top half and Mary and the grouped apostles in the lower half. This geometry gives the icon a beautiful sense of symmetry and balance. There is normally very little in the way of landscape shown in the icon, with the gold of heaven being the dominant background. What landscape is shown is rocky and hilly (Mary is often shown on a small rocky mound) to show that we are on a mountain. Sometimes a few olive trees are included to indicate that we are on the Mount of Olives, the traditional site of the ascension.

The ascended Christ is shown enthroned in heaven. His hand is raised in blessing and He often holds a book or a scroll. The book is closed indicating that His time of teaching has come to an end and He, as king of the universe, is preparing to judge the world. He is shown in a mandorla or in concentric circles. If He is shown in a mandorla, the background is dark to indicate that Christ has returned to the eternal mystery of God which, in a sense, He has never left. The concentric circles indicate the perfect harmony of heaven, and that Christ has passed beyond the spheres of our existence. He is attended by two or more angels who are always shown outside the mandorla or circle, indicating that Christ has returned into the heart of God's mystery where they are unable to go.

In the lower half of the icon we have the central figure of Mary surrounded by two angels. As has been previously noted, Mary is calm, elevated above the apostles and with her arms open in an embracing gesture, either showing the ascended Christ to the world or reaching out to the viewer. In most cases, she is shown looking directly at the viewer. In contrast, the apostles are shown in a considerable state of agitation. They are amazed. Some of them look towards the ascended Christ, some at each other and some at Mary. These are not yet the leaders of the Church. It is Mary who is the spirit bearer at this time, who is central. She is framed by the dominant figures of the two angels who are looking at the apostles and pointing to Christ in heaven. Their gaze is outwards, towards the world, in a clear act of commissioning - sending on a mission. Once again the icon reinforces the emphasis of the scriptural texts.

> After fulfilling for us your plan of redemption and joining the
> things of earth with those of heaven, O Christ our God, You
> gloriously ascended without abandoning us, but remained with
> us forever and reassured all who love you by telling them:
> 'Behold, I am with you: no one has power against you'.[301]

---

[301] Raya and De Vinck, *Byzantine Daily Worship*, 881.

Pentecost (The Fiftieth Day of Easter)

> *When the day of Pentecost had come, they were all together in one place. And suddenly from heaven there came a sound like the rush of a violent wind, and it filled the entire house where they were sitting. Divided tongues, as of fire, appeared among them. All of them were filled with the Holy Spirit and began to speak in other languages, as the Spirit gave them ability.*
> *Acts 2:1-4*

One of the most interesting things about the icon of Pentecost, or *The Descent of the Holy Spirit*, is that there are two of them with quite different forms. One major difference is the presence or absence of Mary in the middle of the assembled Apostles. Other more minor differences are the way in which the apostles are arranged and the presence or absence of the figure of Cosmos in the bottom of the Icon. The earliest portrayals of Pentecost show Mary seated in the centre of the circle of apostles with a tongue of flame above each head.[302] In portrayals of this kind, Mary is presented as the Mother of the Church, and there is a clear link with the icon of the Ascension. Starting in the ninth century, a different form of the icon started to develop where Mary was absent and the figure now known as *Cosmos* started to appear.[303] Although it has been a matter of considerable controversy ever since, this second form has come to be accepted as the standard icon of the feast in Orthodox Churches.[304]

Neither of the icons is particularly true to the scriptural account. In Acts, the descent of the Spirit is a matter of great commotion. There is a great rush of wind and the apostles charge out, so excited that some of the spectators believe that they are drunk. In both icons, the apostles are calm and seated in orderly fashion. Also, characters who could not possibly have been at the historical event – Paul and the evangelists – are shown in the place of some of the apostles who were most certainly present. Once again, neither icon is truly an icon of the event as portrayed in scripture; rather, they are icons of the Church's understanding of the meaning and significance of the event.

This is perhaps the basic difference between these icons and the portrayals of Pentecost in western religious art. Western religious art has tried to illustrate the event as given in Acts. There was little theological content. This is probably why Mary is always shown as present in western images of Pentecost, her presence is

---

[302] Onasch and Schnieper, *Icons*, 189.

[303] Onasch and Schnieper, *Icons*, 189.

[304] For a full, if polemic, discussion of the controversy see L. Ouspensky, 1987, "Iconography of the Descent of the Holy Spirit", *St Vladimir's Theological Quarterly*, 31 (1987): 309-347. It is interesting to note that in this paper, as elsewhere, the Roman Catholic Church is invoked as pivotal in a an Orthodox iconography controversy of which it was probably only barely aware and into which it certainly had no input.

strongly implied in scripture: "…they were all together in one place."[305] Confusion can be generated when such art is considered as if it were the same as a theologically dense Icon.

The later icon, the one without Mary (see Figure 10.3) which has come to be accepted as the Orthodox standard, is more properly considered as an icon of the Liturgy of Pentecost, and to fully understand the icon we must consider its place in the liturgical year. The icon used on Pentecost Sunday is actually an icon of the Trinity. The icon of the Descent of the Holy Spirit is used on the following Monday. The icon should thus be seen in a Trinitarian context. It is the final phase of the action of the Trinity to save the world and bring it to its proper completion – its deification. The Father sent the Son into the world and the Son brought about the world's salvation and made it able to receive the Spirit. Now the Spirit comes to the church so that the mission of deification may be completed. This Icon is thus intimately connected to that of the Ascension. The Ascension marked the completion of Christ's earthly mission in the flesh, while Pentecost marks the beginning of His mission, through the Spirit, in His mystical body - the church.

Figure 10.3
Pentecost

---

[305] Acts 2:1.

The contrast is deliberately made with the ascension by leaving out Mary. At the ascension Mary was the Spirit bearer and the centre of the assembled church. Now the apostles have received the Spirit and it is their mission to teach the rest of the world. This is shown by the twelve scrolls held by the figure of Cosmos. The progression is made from the Ascension, where the apostles are agitated and confused, to Pentecost where they, calmly and in proper order, take up their role as leaders of the church. The change seen in the fishermen is promised to the rest of the world.

The icon also portrays the unity and universality of the church. There is no obvious hierarchy among the gathered apostles, although Peter and Paul, at the top of the arc of apostles, are drawn larger than the others. That all the apostles are shown as equals is intended to show the unity of the church. Paul and the evangelists, representatives of the church not present at the historical event, are included to show the universality of the church. Here, the gift of many tongues brings about unity and calm. This is in contrast to the discord of Babel.[306] There is a sense of completion. The circle has been closed and the final phase in man's long story of salvation is about to begin.

> Blessed art Thou, O Christ our God, who have filled the fishermen with wisdom by sending down the Holy Spirit upon them and who, through them, have united the world. Glory to You, O Lover of Mankind![307]

> When the Most High came down and confused the tongues (in Babel), He divided the nations; but when He distributed the tongues of fire at Pentecost, He called all men to unity. Wherefore we glorify the Holy Spirit with one accord.[308]

In the icon, the Apostles are shown sitting in an elongated arch around the central axis of the icon. That they are in a room is shown by an architectural background draped with red cloth. They are shown in reverse perspective with figures of Peter and Paul, at the top of the arch, drawn larger than the others, perhaps indicating that they are held in greater honour. There is, however, no real hierarchy. All are equal although they may have different tasks. The evangelists, for example, are shown holding books or scrolls.

On the same central axis at the top of the icon there is a dark, partial circle rimmed with gold and with twelve golden rays extending from it. This represents God in His mystery. The partial nature of the circle indicates that God extends far beyond

---

[306] Gen 11:7-9.

[307] Raya and De Vinck, *Byzantine Daily Worship*, 890.

[308] Raya and de Vinck, *Byzantine Daily Worship*, 891.

our understanding, just as the circle extends well beyond the frame of the icon. The twelve rays are the Spirit descending on the assembled apostles. In many icons, the presence of the Spirit is further indicated by tongues of flame over the heads of the apostles, although in some cases this is either vestigial or left out completely. The Spirit is not represented directly in the image, in contrast to some western images where the Spirit is represented by a dove. At the top of the arch, Peter and Paul look at each other across an empty space. In this empty space the Spirit is present. This empty space is the only direct indication of the Spirit and this is one of the reasons for deleting Mary since, in the older icons; she occupies this space.

In a dark arch at the Apostles feet there is the figure of an old man, crowned and clad in royal robes. He holds open a cloth containing twelve scrolls to indicate the teaching authority of the Apostles. He stands in the darkness caused by the sin and ignorance of this world. This figure is normally identified as Cosmos, and he is a personification of the world. The crown and the robes are the empty glory of pride, and he is made old by the weight of sin. The figure was originally a representation of the gentile peoples of the world.[309] He is at the bottom of the same central axis along which the Spirit descends to the Apostles, indicating that the Spirit is not coming to the Apostles or to the Church for their own sake, but for the sake of the world still lost in the darkness of sin. The means of his salvation is shown by the twelve scrolls he holds: the teaching of the Apostles.

This figure is sometimes identified as the prophet Joel, since Joel was held to have prophesied the descent of the Spirit.[310] When this identification is made, the reference is once again to completion. The action of the Spirit has fulfilled the prophecy and law of the Old Testament.

The icon has a strong symmetry around a vertical central axis. Everything in the Icon is arranged around this axis which gives a strong verticality to the Icon's geometry. It is this verticality which gives the sense of the descent of the Spirit.

---

[309] Onasch and Schnieper, *Icons*, 189.
[310] Joel 2:28-29.

CHAPTER ELEVEN

FUNCTION OF ICONS IN THE CHURCH

E_ikon_ is the Greek word used in the Septuagint version of the Hebrew Scriptures to describe the fact that human beings are created in the image and likeness of God. An 'icon' has come to mean a religious image that plays a unique and important role in Orthodox Christian worship and doctrine.

In the Byzantine Christian approach to the mysteries of the Christian faith, the heavenly world and the earthly world are closely related and entwined. The humblest believer can experience God's power and mercy in various ways, whether through acts of nature or healing miracles, or in the sacramental rites of the Church. The icon plays an important role in the life of the believer. At baptism, the newly-baptised is given an icon of the patron saint whose name he or she receives. At marriage, the fathers of the spouses bless them with the gift of icons. At an Orthodox believer's burial their baptismal icon and that of the Blessed Virgin is carried in front of the funeral procession. Also, Orthodox people most often place an icon at the threshold of their house as an invitation to the guest to lift their hearts heavenward. It tells the guest that they are entering the home of a believer. Icons are thus present in some way at every significant moment throughout one's lifetime.

The Icon in the Church

When one enters an Orthodox church covered with frescoes and icons of Christ, angels and all the saints, one cannot feel alone. The believer becomes aware that she is a participant in a great family of the saints, indeed, in the communion of the saints. Their silent, steady gaze speaks of the interior life in Christ. Just as a member of the family is embraced, the offering of candles, lit in honour of Christ and the saints, whose icons are then reverently kissed, so the family ethos is manifested.

St Maximus the Confessor saw the church building itself as a icon of mankind in the cosmos. According to him, the _nave_ is an image of the visible world, the _sanctuary_ an image of the world of the mind. These worlds are joined together by the _cupola_, the sphere above the firmament, a circle, the perfect figure and a visible sign of spiritual unity. The harmonious aggregate of the three parts corresponds to the human composite: body, soul and spirit.[311]

As an aid to meditation, the frescoes and the icons dispose us to contemplate the unseen world. We are constantly reminded that the House of God reflects the cosmic order. The ground level represents our world, the earth, while the ceilings

---

[311] See Dom Julian Stead, _The Church, the Liturgy and the Soul of Man: The Mystagogia of St. Maximus the Confessor_ (Still River, MA: St. Bede's Publications, 1982). "God's holy Church [is] a figure and image of the entire world composed of visible and invisible essences because, like it, it contains both unity and diversity." St. Maximos, _Mystagogia_. 2.

represent the celestial world, heaven, and the sanctuary unites the two worlds.

Regarded in strict theological terms, not as objects of devotion in themselves, but as windows into the divine realm, icons are kissed and venerated at different times during the *Divine Liturgy*. It is important to remember however that icons occupy a particular place in the hierarchy of holy objects within the church. One would not venerate an icon when the Eucharistic elements are being carried in or consecrated. The icon may occupy a central place within a sacramental act such as confession or an anointing with holy oil.[312]

The earliest icons were believed to have been painted at the time of Christ. Perhaps the most famous one is of the Blessed Virgin, which, according to legend, was painted by the Evangelist Luke. Then later on, in the sixth century, another legend relates the story of a King Abgar of Edessa (sometimes rendered Avgar), who fell ill and sent a message to the Saviour, begging him to come and cure him. Jesus could not come personally, but sent a miraculous image of his Holy Face imprinted on a cloth.[313] Thus traditionally, icons were not only countenanced and blessed by the Lord, but the first one was made by him and of him. Whether this story is true in the historical sense or in the practical meaning of truth, the fact remains that we venerate icons as representations of the reality, but we do not worship them.

Portable icons were usually painted on wooden panels, although they might also be fashioned in ivory, mosaic or enamel. [314]Pigment was applied to a wooden panel, usually cypress, which had been strengthened with cloth and gesso to prevent splits or cracks. In the earliest icons that survive at St. Catherine's Monastery in Sinai, a wax encaustic has been used. Later pigments mixed with an egg tempera medium were more commonly employed in the manufacture of icons. Gold leaf was applied liberally to the background and the finished painting was protected with varnish.

The Hierarchy of Icons in the Church

From the ninth century onward, official rules prescribe the choice and disposition of the iconography to be painted on the walls and ceilings of the churches. Accordingly, the icon of Christ Pantocrator, Master of the visible and invisible universe, occupies the large cupola of the church. It is given such a prominent position because it serves as a reminder that Jesus Christ rules over all creation. It suggests a window on Heaven and constitutes the summit within the hierarchy of the imagery. In the icon of Christ Pantocrator, his hand of blessing expresses the Trinity and the two natures of the Chalcedonian Definition (see Figure One). The

---

[312] Mary Cunningham, *Faith in the Byzantine World* (Oxford: Lion Publishing, 2002), 101.

[313] The Latin Church has a similar legend in which Veronica (from the Latin for true image) wipes the face of the tortured Jesus as he is carrying his cross on the way to his crucifixion. Onto the woman's cloth Jesus is said to have miraculously left his impression. The cloth was discovered by the mother of Constantine, Helena when she went looking for archaeological discoveries in the fourth century.

[314] Cunningham, Faith *in the Byzantine World*, 163.

elongated fingers point towards the heart as a reminder of the Kingdom of Heaven within. Around the head of the Christ Pantocrator there may be a halo, in which is sometimes written the Greek initials of Christ's name (IC XC). The halo may also contain the image of a cross within its border. This image of Christ developed very early in Church history, the most famous one being the Pantocrator of the sixth century found at St. Catherine's Monastery, Sinai. The Pantocrator Christ balances the double paradox of Christ as Judge and Saviour and Christ as God and man. This Pantocrator Christ also has a book in his hand, sometimes open, sometimes closed. A symbol of revelation, the book signifies Christ as Judge or Saviour or Teacher, depending on the text portrayed. The tunic and cloak worn by the Pantocrator Christ symbolise the two natures of Christ, both divine and human.

> On the vaulting of the sanctuary is portrayed the *Theotokos*, the Mother of God, our "Bridge" between Heaven and earth. Surrounding the altar like a protecting wall, the apse pictures the celestial liturgy of the Angels on the upper section of the wall, and on the lower level the eternal communion of the apostles. Above the church exit you generally see aa fresco of the Dormition of the Theotokos, or of the last Judgement- vivid reminders for the faithful as they return home. The iconography of the saints occupies the remainder of ordinary mural space... Those icons exposed on the "proskynetaria", or icon stands, are there for the immediate veneration of the faithful, who neither kneel nor genuflect upon entering the church; instead they make the sign of the Cross – up to three times, in honour of the Most Holy Trinity. Standing,they recite a short prayer with head bowed before the icons, which they venerate with a kiss: first, the icon of Christ, next, that of the Theotokos, and then ordinarily the icon of the feast-day or of the liturgical cycle, placed in evidence in the middle of the church...[315]

The Iconostasis

During the seventh and eighth centuries, the celebration of the *Divine Liturgy* came to be regarded more and more as a sacred mystery and consecrated behind the templon screen, or iconostasis and administered only to those who were prepared.[316]

> The term *iconostasis* means simply a partition covered with icons. Of reather late origin, it attained its classical form in the fifteenth century. In the churches of early Christianity, the sanctuary was separated from the nave by a low screen, latticed

---

[315] Quenot, *The Icon*, 46-47.
[316] Cunningham, *Faith in the Byzantine World*, 114.

grill, or a low, solid wall. With the increase in the number of icons
this slowly changed. The icons were first hung onto the grill in
one row, and then on a second. Finally, we find up to five rows
or tiers, thus giving the iconostasis the form that we recognize
today. Its evolution and development raised it to the vault, both
isolating the priest and at the same time blocking the complete
view of the frescoes on the sanctuary walls. The solution was to
use on the iconostasis itself the same iconographic plan as for
the cupola, the sanctuary and the nave... By no means a barrier,
the iconostasis is, positively speaking, the maximal expression
of all that the icon can reveal to us visually. Behind it there
is nothing to be seen. Why? Simply because the wondrous
mystery that is celebrated there could never be situated on our
human, visual level, so to speak; such a wondrous mystery is
perceived perceived not by human eyes, but only by the soul in
communion. [317]

The full iconostasis is an expression of the whole of Salvation history. Each tier
has its own central icon on which the other icons are focused. The screen is an
expression of Eucharistic theology and it brings together the idea of the Body of
Christ as bread and wine, and the idea of the Body of Christ as the Church.

The iconostasis has three doors (see Figure Two): the *North Door* on the left, leads
to the sacrificial table where the bread and wine are prepared for the Eucharist; the
South Door leads to the deaconry and usually has angels on it, because the deacon
has the symbolic role of an angel in the Liturgy. The most important doors are the
central doors, known as the *Royal Doors*; only a priest may pass through them,
and then only at certain times, key moments in the Liturgy. These Royal doors
symbolise the crossing-over point between two worlds, the intersection of heaven
and earth, and they always contain the same icons: the Annunciation, the Four
Evangelists, and above the doors hangs the icon of the Last Supper. These three
icons represent the meeting of heaven and earth in the Incarnation, in the Word, and
in the Sacrament. The icon of the Last Supper shows Christ giving communion to
the Apostles and hangs above the place where the priest distributes the elements,
thus stressing the apostolic continuity. On the edges of the Royal Doors are icons of
the two Church Fathers, the Liturgists St John Chrysostom and St Basil.

---

[317] Quenot, M. *The Icon*, 47-48.

↑
Royal door
The Annunciation and the Four Evangelists
This door, called "Royal," symbolizes the entry into the Kingdom of God.
The Annunciation marks the beginning of our salvation.

The Old Testament Church (period under the law):
  1a. From Adam to Moses (The Patriarchs);
  1b. From Moses to Christ (The Prophets).

The New Testament Church (period of grace):
  2. Icons of the 12 Great Feasts
  3. Deisis = intercession. Prayer of the Church
      for the world.

The essential row: it is the accomplishment of the three upper rows.

Other Saints	St Peter	Archangel Gabriel	The Mother of God	Christ	St John the Baptist	Archangel Michael	St Paul	Other Saints

4. Objects of direct personal veneration: kisses, candles, incense.

Figure Two
Iconostasis [318]

The iconostasis teaches that salvation is a two way process. God descends to humanity; this descent is foreshadowed by the patriarchs, foretold in the prophets and fulfilled in the New Testament. Secondly, salvation requires human cooperation towards God, which happens in the preaching of the Gospel and the celebration of

---

[318] Quenot, *The Icon*, 49.

the Eucharist. When the descent of God and the ascent of humanity meet, it will culminate in the transfiguration of all creation in the Realm of God. This is the true meaning of the iconostasis and why some writers like Ouspensky object very strongly to any suggestion that the Orthodox Church should return to the simple balustrade of the early church. Michael Quenot claims that the iconostasis is not a screen because the Eucharistic mystery cannot be seen, therefore it cannot be hidden. The iconostasis reveals rather than conceals the Eucharist.

> The iconostasis is thus not limited to simply recapitulating the entire economy of salvation for our eyes and our senses, though this is already a fact of great importance; it suggests a spiritual passage into another world which remains invisible to our earthly eyes. In other words, it symbolises that boundary between the sensual world and the spiritual world. Beyond its didactic intent and purpose, the iconostasis invites us to a spiritual communion with the Celestial Church. It serves to emphasise that essential bond between the sacrament of the glorious Body of Christ, the Eucharist – and the icon, representation of His transfigured Body.[319]

Portable Icons

Icons keep the fact of the Incarnation alive for us. Christ, in his tender love for humanity, took upon himself a human form, real flesh and blood. Icons continue for us the immediate promise of the Incarnation. They remind us of his actual presence. To prevent idolatry and superstition the Church has striven to preserve the purity of the stylised icon. Nothing is permitted that might allow a 'realism' that might lead one to forget that icons only representations. They are not the reality that they represent. To be authentic, icons must have the blessing of the Church.

The Fathers of the Seventh Ecumenical Council (787 CE) warned against worshipping icons. They should not be treated as idols, but as paths that lead to what they represent. They can evoke the presence of God in church, home, or wayside and are invitations to a focused seeing while one is praying. Icons are bridges to Christ; links to the saints, and reminders of pivotal events in the history of salvation. Icons bring one into the presence of that which they represent. Greatness becomes present to one when an icon lifts one's mind to God.

Blessing of Icons

The form of Blessing of an icon varies from one tradition to another. In the Russian Catholic Church, an icon is simply placed on the altar during the *Divine Liturgy*. No particular prayers are said to bless the icon. In the Melkite Byzantine Church,

---

[319] Quenot, *The Icon*, 48.

if a Bishop blesses the icon, he anoints the four sides of it with Holy Chrism, and then says the following prayer:

> Master, our Almighty King, Father of our Lord and Saviour Jesus Christ, You gave orders to your servant Moses to sketch a picture of a Cherub in the Holy Tent, and from this, we took the custom of sketching icons as a remembrance of those whom they represent. Therefore, we pray to You O Lord our King, to send the grace of your Holy Spirit, together with your angel, on this holy icon so that every prayer which is offered to You through this icon may be accepted by the grace, mercy and compassion of your only-begotten Son, our Lord and Saviour Jesus Christ, the Lover of Mankind.[320]

However if a priest blesses an icon, he says the prayer first and then sprinkles it with holy water, each time saying:

> May this Icon be blessed + in the name of the Father and the Son and of the Holy Spirit. Amen.[321]

In the Greek Orthodox Archdiocese of America, the *Blessing and Hallowing of Icons*[322] contains the following prayers:

> O Lord our God, Who created us after Your own Image and Likeness; Who redeems us from our former corruption of the ancient curse through Your manfriending Christ, Who took upon Himself the form of a servant and became man, Who having taken upon Himself our likeness remade Your Saints of the first dispensation, and through Whom also we are refashioned in the Image of Your pure blessedness;
>
> Your Saints we venerate as being in Your Image and Likeness, and we adore and glorify You as Creator;
>
> Wherefore we pray You, send forth Your blessing upon this Icon, and with the sprinkling of hallowed water
>
> Bless and make holy this Icon unto your glory, honour and remembrance of Your Saint (N);
>
> And grant that this sanctification will be to all who venerate this

---

[320] *Byzantine Melkite Euchologion*   (Jounieh Lebanon: St Paul's Printing Press, 1972), 179.

[321] *Byzantine Melkite Euchologion*, 180.

[322] "The Blessing and Harrowing of Icons" http://goach.org/en/chapel/liturgical_texts/icon_blessing.asp [accessed 16 September, 2004]

Icon of Saint (N), and send up their prayer unto You standing before it:

> Through the grace and bounties and love of Your Only-Begotten Son, with Whom You are blessed together with Your All-Holy, Good and Life-creating Spirit; both now and ever, unto ages of ages.

Sprinkling cross fashion the Icon with Holy Water, the priest says:

> Hallowed and blessed is this Icon of St. (N) by the grace of the Holy Spirit, through the sprinkling of Holy Water: in the name of the Father (+) and of the Son (+) and of the Holy Spirit (+), Amen.

The prayers for the blessing of icons are not only revealing in their theological significance, but also they are quite beautiful prayers. They take us out of this world into a realm still temporal, but outside change.

Western Christianity's Rediscovery of the Icon

One must always remember that an icon is not just a beautiful picture to gaze at. The icon is a sacrament for the Christian East. More precisely, it is the vehicle of a personal presence. An image that has been painted following traditional rules, and has been blessed by a priest, becomes a "miraculous icon". "Miraculous" here means exactly that the icon is charged with a presence. An icon is an icon when it is a painting on a wooden panel, in tempera colours, depicting persons or events and painted according to traditional iconographical rules or instructions. These rules or instructions have been followed for many, many centuries and may be found in Manuals for Iconographers.

A recent Westernised theology of the icon interprets the Pantocrator icon (of Sixth Century Constantinople, preserved at St Catherine's Sinai) as depicting the dual aspects of God's parental love, one side of the face depicting the paternal, conditional love of a father, whilst the other side of the face portraying God's maternal, unconditional love. This is an ingenious but anachronistic theologising, quite alien to the vision of the original iconographer and which would have made no sense to him. Besides, most or all human faces are not symmetrical. Doubtless the model used by this iconographer of the Sinai Pantocrator had an asymmetrical face. But that is not to say that Jesus did not also have a slightly asymmetrical face.

CHAPTER TWELVE

ANASTASIS: ICON, TEXT AND THEOLOGICAL VISION

The fresco of the Anastasis (1310-1320) in the monastery of the Holy Saviour in the Fields, Constantinople, is one of the supreme works of Christian theological art (see Figure 12.1) if not 'the' supreme work. This chapter will explore its theological foundations, the historical developments of the image, and present a stylistic exegesis. This supreme work, executed on the cusp of the City's doom, illustrates the enduring vitality of the Greek patristic vision, with a power that it still exercises today.

Figure 12.1
Anastasis, Church of the Holy Saviour in the Fields,
Constantinople

Theological Foundations
In Western Christianity the Resurrection is sometimes depicted with a victorious Christ standing boldly with a staff pole bearing a red cross on a white background. Christ is shown rising from the tomb, with soldiers or angels at his sides. This western-styled image was introduced into the Eastern Church in post-Byzantine times and is sometimes used in eastern churches. Some Orthodox scholars (e.g. Kontoglou and Uspenski) consider this image unacceptable because it is naturalistic and strictly speaking not "according to the Scriptures." In the East two images are used to depict the Resurrection: the Anastasis Icon (The Harrowing of Hell), and

the Myrrh-bearing Women. Quite clearly, the source of inspiration for the Myrrh-bearing Women is Scriptural (Mt 28:1-10; Mk 16:1-8; Lk 24:1-12; Jn 20:1-10) but the source of inspiration for the more frequent representation of the Resurrection in the East, the Anastasis, is not as certain, but the teaching that the Lord "descended into hell" to liberate the waiting dead, appear in the earliest creeds.

Whilst disagreeing about the literary source of the image, all the scholars agree that it was the ongoing controversy concerning the precise relationship between Christ's human and divine natures during his death and Resurrection that led artists to shy away from depicting Christ at any moment during his dying and death. It was not until after these questions had been resolved in the late seventh century, at the Sixth Ecumenical Council (680-681) and the Council of Trullo (691), that artists began to represent Christ's death, entombment and Resurrection. The earliest surviving versions of the Anastasis are those of eighth century Rome. Then over the following six hundred years the image evolved into the splendour we have before us, the Anastasis of the Church of the Holy Saviour in the Fields, Istanbul.

Scriptural References

There is no reference to the Anastasis event in the four canonical Gospels. "Customarily art scholars have tended to explain this icon on the basis of the Apocryphal Gospel of Nicodemus (or the Acts of Pilate) of the fourth or fifth centuries in which Christ's descent into hell and its harrowing are described quite dramatically".[323] However, there is clear evidence in both the Hebrew and Christian Scriptures, of the Anastasis event.

Psalm 16 for example:

> So my heart rejoices, my soul delights, my body too, will rest
> secure, For you will not leave my soul in hell, neither will you
> allow your Holy One to see corruption (Ps 16:9-10).

The case of Jonah as precursor sign of Christ's Resurrection was given to the Christian community by Christ himself:

> For as Jonah remained in the belly of the sea-monster for three
> days and three nights, so will the Son of Man be in the heart of
> the earth for three days and three nights (Matt 12:40).

---

[323] George Dragas, *Understanding the Resurrection through Christ's Descent into Hades* http://www.orthodoxnews. netfirms.com/170/Understanding%20the%20Resurrection.htm [accessed 23 June, 2005], 3.

Paul writes to the Ephesians:

> When it says, 'he went up,' it must mean that he had gone down
> to the deepest levels of the earth. The one who went down is
> none other than the one who went up above all the heavens to
> fill all things (Ephesians 4:9).

In 1 Peter, a paragraph (3:18-4:6) contains the elements of an ancient profession of
faith: death of Christ, his descent into hell, his resurrection, his enthronement at the
right hand of God the Father, and as the judge of the living and dead.

> Christ himself died once and for all for sins, the upright for the
> sake of the guilty, to lead us to God. In the body he was put to
> death, in the spirit he was raised to life, and in the spirit, he went
> to preach to the spirits in prison (1 Pet 3:18).

Later in the same Letter of Peter:

> And this was why the gospel was brought to the dead as well, so
> that, though in their bodies they had undergone the judgement
> that faces all humanity, in their spirit they might enjoy the life
> of God (1 Pet 4:6).

Patristic Evidence

Apart from the Scriptural references, the earliest evidence of a literary source for
the Anastasis comes from the latter part of the first century, in what are known as
the Odes of Solomon. They were almost certainly composed in Syriac, probably
in the latter part of the first century, and very likely in northern Syria, that is in
Antioch, Edessa or some nearby centre. Their tone is predominately Jewish,
although there are many Christian overtones. There are many parallels, in terms
and ideas, with the Gospel of John, but scholars have discounted any dependence
on that work. Even greater though are the parallels with certain of the Dead Sea
Scrolls, especially the Thanksgiving Hymns, and the Odes of Solomon as a whole
are clearly modelled on the Davidic Psalms. Odes 22 and 42 are thought to contain
references to the image of the Anastasis.

ODE 22

(From the *Odes of Solomon*)

[1]He who caused me to descend from on high,
    and to ascend from the regions below;
[2]And He who gathers what is in the Middle,
    and throws them to me;
[3]He who scattered my enemies, and my adversaries:
[4]He who gave me authority over bonds,
    so that I might unbind them;
[5]He who overthrew by my hands the dragon with seven heads,
    and set me at his roots that I might destroy his seed;
[6]You were there and helped me,
    and in every place Your name surrounded me.
[7]Your right hand destroyed his evil venom,
    and Your hand levelled the Way
    for those who believe in You.
[8]And it chose them from the graves,
    and separated them from the dead ones.
[9]It took dead bones and covered them with flesh.
[10]But they were motionless, so It gave them energy for life.
[11]Incorruptable was Your Way and Your face;
    You have brought Your world to corruption,
    that everything might be resolved and renewed.
[12]And the foundation of everything is Your rock.
    And upon it You have built Your kingdom,
    And it became the dwelling-place of the holy ones.
    Alleluia![324]

ODE 42

(From the Odes of Solomon)

[1]I extended my hands and approached my Lord,
    For the expansion of my hands is His sign.
[2]And my extension is the upright cross,
    that was lifted up on the way of the Righteous One.
[3]And I became useless to those who knew me not,
    because I shall hide myself from those who possessed me not.
[4]And I will be with those who love me.
[5]All my persecutors have died, and they sought me,
    they who declared against me, because I am living.

---

[324] James Charlesworth, trans., *The Odes of Solomon*, http://www.misericordia.edu/users/davies/thomas/odes.htm .
[accessed 14 June, 2005]

⁶The I arose and am with them, and will speak by their mouths.
⁷For they have rejected those who persecute them;
       and I threw over them the yolk of my love.
⁸Like the arm of the bridegroom over the bride,
       so is my yoke over those who know me.
⁹And as the bridal chamber is spread out by the bridal pair's home,
       so is my love by those who believe in me.
¹⁰I was not rejected although I was considered to be so,
       and I did not perish although they thought it of me.
¹¹Sheol saw me and was shattered, and Death ejected me
       and many with me.
¹²I have been vinegar and bitterness to it;
       and I went down with it as far as its depth.
¹³Then the feet and the head it released,
       because it was not able to endure my face.
¹⁴And I made a congregation of living among his dead;
       and I spoke with them by living lips
       in order that my word may not be unprofitable.
¹⁵And those who had died ran towards me;
       and said "Son of God, have pity on us.
¹⁶And deal with us according to Your kindness
       and bring us out from the bonds of darkness.
¹⁷And open for us the door by which we may come out to You;
       for we perceive that our death does not touch You.
¹⁸May we also be saved with You because You are our Saviour."
¹⁹Then I heard their voice, and place their faith in my heart.
²⁰And I placed my name upon their head,
       because they are free and they are mine.[325]

At the beginning of the second century, the Church Fathers introduced the subject of Christ's journey to the underworld. There is a treasury of Patristic texts which shed light on the mystery of the Anastasis and all the Fathers of the Church touched on this most important subject in their writings. Canon 9 of the Fifth Ecumenical Council (Constantinople 553) condemned anyone who denied the Descent of Christ into Hell and his ascension from it as Victor into the Highest Heaven. The Seventh Ecumenical Council (Nicaea 787) stated that Christ:

> "spoiled Hell and delivered the captives who were kept there from all ages".[326]

Another very early Patristic reference to it occurs early in the second century in the Epistle of Ignatius (50-107) to the Trallians:

---

[325] Charlesworth, *The Odes of Solomon.*
[326] George Dragas, *Understanding the Resurrection*

For says the Scripture, 'Many of the saints that slept arose,' their graves being opened. He descended, indeed, into Hades alone, but he arose accompanied by a multitude; and rent asunder that means of separation which had existed from the beginning of the world, and cast down its partition-wall. He also rose again in three days, the Father raising him up.[327]

From the middle of the second century, Melito of Sardis (died 180) refers to Christ as:

"a unique sun from heaven Who appeared to those dead in Hell and to those living in the world".[328]

Furthermore, in a letter, Melito of Sardis writes:

The Lord, though he was God, became man. He suffered for the sake of whose who suffer, he was bound for those in bonds, condemned for the guilty, buried for those who lie in the grave; but he rose from the dead, and cried aloud: "Who will contend with me? Let him confront me." I have freed the condemned, brought the dead back to life, raised men from their graves. Who has anything to say against me? I, he said, am the Christ; I have destroyed death, triumphed over the enemy, trampled hell underfoot, bound the strong one, and taken men up to the heights of heaven: I am the Christ.[329]

Saint Hippolytus (170-235) commenting on Deuteronomy 33:26 says:

He is the One Who pulled up from the lowest Hell the first man who was from the earth and had been lost, having been held captive by the bonds of death. He is the One Who descended from above and brought above him who was down below. He is the One Who preached the Gospel to the dead and redeemed the souls, Who became the resurrection of those that had been buried ... He was the Helper of the man who had been conquered; the One Who assimilated Himself with him ... the Noble One Who wants to restore to the slave to freedom through His Own obedience .[330]

The Apostles' Creed, a formula containing in brief statements, or "articles," the fundamental tenets of Christian belief, was developed between the second and ninth centuries, although some scholars claim that it was in its settled form by the fourth century.

---

[327] Alexander Roberts and James Donaldson, *St. Ignatius of Antioch to the Trallians* http://www. earlychristianwritings.com/text/ignatius-trallians-longer.html. [accessed 17 June 2005].

[328] Dragas. *Understanding the Resurrection*, 6.

[329] "St Melito of Sardis" http://www.catholic-forum.com/saints/saintm18.html [accessed 30 June, 2005].

[330] Dragas *Understanding the Resurrection*, 6.

I believe in God, the Father almighty,
creator of heaven and earth.

I believe in Jesus Christ, God's only Son, our Lord,
who was conceived by the Holy Spirit,
born of the Virgin Mary,
suffered under Pontius Pilate,
was crucified, died, and was buried;
he descended into hell.
On the third day he rose again;
he ascended into heaven,
he is seated at the right hand of the Father,
and he will come again to judge the living and the dead.

I believe in the Holy Spirit,
the holy catholic church,
the communion of saints,
the forgiveness of sins,
the resurrection of the body,
and the life everlasting. Amen.

Apocryphon of Nicodemus also known as the Acts of Pilate

The first part of the text, containing the story of the Passion and Resurrection, is not earlier than the fourth century. Its object is to furnish testimony to the Resurrection. Part II is the story of the Descent into Hell. It is probably older than Part I, and is thought by the scholars to have been added to Part I, but not before the fifth century. We have the text in three forms: Latin A, Greek and Latin B. Greek copies are rare and it is in Latin that it has chiefly flourished, and has been the parent of versions in every other language. The central idea in Part II, Christ's Descent into Hell, is exceedingly ancient. Second-century writers are full of it. The embellishments, the dialogues of Satan with Hades, which are so dramatic, come in later.

The following table[331] shows the order of the story in the three recensions available to us. Latin A and Greek go together, while Latin B differs.

---

[331] Montague Rhodes James, *The Apocryphal New Testament* (London: Oxford University Press, 1924, 1955), 118.

i. The two men (nameless in Greek) are found and induced to write their story.	i. The two men are found, write their story, and return to their tombs.
ii. The story. A light shines in Hell. Adam, Esaias, Simeon speak (not in B). (In Greek, Abraham and Esaias.) John Baptist comes.	ii. The story. A light shines. A voice: Lift up the gates. Satan has the doors secured.
iii. Seth's story of the oil of mercy.	iii. Dialogue of Hell and Satan (A. iv).
iv. Satan's dialogue with Hell.	iv. Seth's story.
v. First cry: Lift up the gates. David and Isaiah speak. Second Cry. David speaks. Christ enters. (Greek, David speaks only once.)	v. Isaiah and John Baptist (A. ii).
vi. Address of Hell to Christ (not in B). Satan bound.	vi. David and Jeremiah. Satan not allowed to leave hell.
vii. Hell derides Satan.	vii. Cry: Lift up the gates. The good thief appears (A. x). Second cry.
viii. Christ greets Adam and takes all saints out of hell. David, Habacuc, Micheas speak (not in B). (Greek omits the prophecies.)	viii. Doors broken. Christ enters. Satan bound.
ix. They meet Enoch and Elias (not in B.).	ix. Christ greets Adam and Eve (not in A).
x. They meet the thief.	x. Sets up his cross in hell (not in A). Leaves hell.
xi. Conclusion.	xi Conclusion.
xii. The two men vanish, &c.	

The Hodegos, or Guide-Book, of Anastasius Sinaites, a late seventh century text intended to help the Orthodox defend themselves against heretics, contains many references to Christ's descent into Hades.

One of the most beautiful references to the Anastasis event is from the writings of Epiphanius of Cyprus (or Salamis):

> Something strange is happening – there is a great silence on earth today, a great silence and stillness. The whole earth keeps silence because the King is asleep. The earth trembled and is still because God has fallen asleep in the flesh and he has raised up all who have slept ever since the world began. God has died in the flesh and hell trembles with fear.

He has gone to search for our first parent, as for a lost sheep. Greatly desiring to visit those who live in darkness and in the shadow of death, he has gone to free from sorrows the captives Adam and Eve, he who is both God and the son of Eve. The Lord approached them bearing the cross, the weapon that had won him the victory. At the sight of him, Adam, the first man he had created, struck his breast in terror and cried out to everyone: "My Lord be with you all." Christ answered him: "And with your spirit." He took him by the hand and raised him up, saying: "Awake O sleeper, and rise from the dead, and Christ will give you light."

I am you God, who for your sake have become your son. Out of love for you and your descendants I now by my own authority command all who are held in bondage to come forth, all who are in darkness to be enlightened, all who are sleeping to arise. I order you O sleeper, to awake. I did not create you to be held prisoner in hell. Rise from the dead, for I am the life of the dead. Rise up, work of my hands, you who were created in my image. Rise, let us leave this place, for you are in me and I am in you; together we form only one person and we cannot be separated.

For your sake, I, your God, became your son; I, the Lord, took the form of a slave; I, whose hole is above the heavens, descended to the earth and beneath the earth. For your sake, for the sake of man, I became like a man without help, free among the dead. For the sake of you, who left a garden, I was betrayed to the leaders of the Jews in a garden, and I was crucified in a garden.

See on my face the spittle I received in order to restore you to the life I once breathed into you. See there the marks of the blows I received in order to refashion your warped nature in my image. On my back see the marks of the scourging I endured to remove the burden of sin that weighs on your back. See my hands, nailed firmly to a tree, for you who once wickedly stretched out your hand to a tree.

I slept on the cross and a sword pierced my side for you who slept in paradise and brought forth Eve from your side. My side has healed the pain in yours. My sleep will rouse you from your sleep in hell. The sword that pierced me has sheathed the sword that was turned against you.

Rise, Let us leave this place. The enemy led you out of the earthly paradise. I will not restore you to that paradise, but I will enthrone you in heaven. I forbade you the tree that was only a symbol of life, but see – I who am life itself am now one with you. I appointed cherubim to guard you as slaves are guarded, but now I make them worship you as God. The throne formed by my cherubim awaits you, its bearers swift and eager. The bridal chamber is adorned, the banquet is ready, the eternal dwelling places are prepared, the treasure houses of all good things lie open. The kingdom of heaven has been prepared for you from all eternity.[332]

Liturgy of the Hours

The Liturgy of the Hours (or the Daily Offices) has evolved over the whole lifetime of the Church. It is rather difficult to ascertain which came first, the Liturgy of the Hours, or the awareness of the Anastasis event. What is certain however is that there are many references to the Anastasis event in the Liturgies of Great and Holy Saturday in both the Western Latin Church and the Eastern Orthodox Churches.

In the Matins of Great and Holy Saturday

O Messiah, Jesus, My King, the Lord of all,

Whom are you seeking in the depths of hell?

Have you come to free the race of mortal men?

Lo, the Sovereign Ruler Of creation is dead.

Almighty God is laid in a new tomb,

To empty the graves of all their dead.

O Christ, Creator, You were laid within a tomb.

Hell's foundations quaked and trembled, seeing You

Opening the graves of mortal men.

When devouring Hades

Engulfed the Rock of Life,

In great pain he burst asunder,

And the dead, held captive from all ages

Were released.[333]

---

[332] Epiphanius, *From an ancient homily on Holy Saturday*, PG 43, 440-64. See also, *Synaxarion of The Lenten Triodion and Pentecostarion*, ed. David Kidd, and Gabriella Ursache (Rives Junction,MI:HDM, 1999), 160-161.

[333] *Great and Holy Saturday Matins* http://www.ocf.org/OrthodoxPage/prayers/triodion/hwk_sat [accessed 16 June, 2005].

Any or all of these sources may be claimed as *the* source of inspiration for the icon of the *Anastasis*. Each is so theologically rich. Finally, from the writing of Epiphanius of Cyprus, comes this lovely and extraordinary piece written for Vespers for Holy Saturday:

> Yesterday the incarnation was demonstrated,
>
> Today, the authority;
>
> Yesterday the feebleness,
>
> Today, the absolute mastery;
>
> Yesterday the humanity,
>
> Today, the divinity;
>
> Yesterday he was stricken,
>
> Today, he strikes the abode of Hades,
>
> With the lightning of his divinity;
>
> Yesterday he was bound up,
>
> Today, he ties down the tyrant in indissoluble bonds;
>
> Yesterday he was condemned,
>
> Today, he presents freedom to the condemned.[334]

The Genesis and Development of the Image

The icon of the Anastasis – the Descent of Christ into Hell – is a sacred image that was created and developed by Christian artists of the Orthodox Byzantine Church.[335] It is one of the favourite themes in Eastern Christian Art and serves as the traditional Byzantine icon for the Resurrection.[336] According to Anna Kartsonis, the Anastasis image was created in the late seventh century and continued to evolve until it reached its final form in the eleventh century.

Genesis of the Icon: Following Kartsonis

In the Early Christian period the Fathers of the Church discussed, preached and affirmed Christ's Descent into Hell. Although the subject of Christ's Resurrection following his triumph over Death and the raising of Adam and Eve from the dead "had formed part of Byzantine theology and liturgy throughout the Early Christian period" it was not depicted by the artists of the period.[337] In any representation of Christ's Crucifixion and Resurrection in this period the actual moment of Christ's death and Resurrection is only alluded to but never portrayed. In the sixth century

---

[334] *The Triodion*, PG, 43.44OD-44IA

[335] A.D.Kartsonis, *Anastasis: The Making of an Image* (Princeton, New Jersey: Princeton University Press, 1986), 3-4.

[336] Cross, *Eastern Christianity*, 107.

[337] Kartsonis, *Anastasis*, 227.

Syriac representation of the *Crucifixion and Resurrection*, Christ is actually shown alive on the Cross, the two Maries are seen at the empty tomb, and Christ appears to them after the Resurrection.[338]

Kartsonis argues that the artists of the Early Christian period consistently avoided the direct representation of the subject of Christ's Descent into Hell, mainly on account of the Christological difficulties that exist in the depiction of the person of Jesus Christ, true God and true man, at any moment during his death. Since Christ was dead, and his soulless body lay buried in the tomb, at the moment he destroyed Hades and took Adam by the hand from among the dead, these events were not depicted by artists of the period. It was not until after the Sixth Ecumenical Council (680-681) and the Council in Trullo (692) that the attitude of the artists changed.

The Councils' resolution of some of the Christological questions concerning the relationship between Christ's two natures during the various aspects of his death, and the authorized use of the visual arts in the service of the Church and its theological concerns, gave artists the confidence to illustrate the theme of Christ's Death. Hence, in the late seventh century artists began to portray the subject of Christ's Death "in the shape of the representation of the Death of Christ on the cross, the Entombment of his soulless, sightless, and speechless corpse, and the Anastasis [or Resurrection] from Hades through the will and energy of his divinity".[339] It is in this context, according to Kartsonis, that the Anastasis icon was born. Kartsonis uses the late 7th century handbook, the *Hodegos*, to argue that the image was also originally created as a way of defending the Orthodox faith against those (*Monophysites*) who asserted that there was only one nature in Christ (*Monophysitism*).[340]

First Compositional Type

a) Eighth Century

The iconographic nucleus of the three earliest surviving representations of the Anastasis, from eighth century Rome, shows that Christ has just defeated Hades and is focusing his attention on raising Adam out of his sarcophagus. The main characters in all three representations are Christ, Adam, and Hades. They determine the content of the action and the image. In the fresco on the doorway to the Palatine ramp in S. Maria Antiqua for example, Christ dominates the composition (see Figure 12.2). He is enclosed in a mandorla of light and his only two contacts with the surrounding material world are with Adam and Hades. He holds Adam's limp hand which is inside the mandorla and he tramples Hades with the tip of his foot which is outside the mandorla.

---

[338] K.Corrigan, "Book Review," in *The Art Bulletin*, Vol.71, No.2 (1989), 312.

[339] Kartsonis, *Anastasis*, 228.

[340] Corrigan, "Book Review," 312.

Figure 12.2
The Anastasis (after Wilpert), S. Maria Antiqua, Rome

Adam is an old man who rises limply out of his sarcophagus. He is not taking an active part in Christ's forceful effort to lift him from his sarcophagus. Adam is totally reliant "on the will and energy"[341] displayed by Christ. On the other hand, the dark muscular figure of Hades is still trying to stop Adam from rising out of the sarcophagus, even though Hades is restrained by Christ's trampling foot.

The primary theme in these eighth century images of the Anastasis is the action of Christ in the underworld. Christ raises Adam after trampling Hades, "whose hold on Adam is in the process of being broken".[342] The iconography provides "a forceful illustration of the will and energy of Christ's divinity in action".[343] The mandorla of light which envelopes Christ underlines this divine action since it stands for the light of Christ's divinity.

b) Ninth Century
In the ninth century Western examples of the Anastasis, which descended from the same iconographic group as those in eighth century Rome, the focus of the

---

[341] Kartsonis, *Anastasis*, 71.
[342] Kartsonis, *Anastasis*, 71.
[343] Kartsonis, *Anastasis*, 71.

image is on the rescue of Adam from the dark and sunless place (*tenebrae*) of the underworld. Christ's direction has changed. His effort in raising Adam is not as forceful and he appears to be moving into a dark cave while drawing Adam out of it. Hades is absent, and if he is represented, he "lies flat on the ground incapable of any meaningful resistance to Christ's power".[344] The late ninth century S.Clemente Anastasis in Rome, highlights the development of particular aspects of the story. The darkness of Hades is stressed and the addition of fires and floating human body parts in Hades portrays the underworld as Hell. The replacement of the scroll in Christ's hands with the long staffed cross emphasizes the role of Christ's Passion in bringing about salvation. Finally, the inclusion of the portrait of a cleric "reasserts the broader message of the raising of the dead".[345]

The Anastasis in the Chapel of S.Zeno in S. Maria Prassede, Rome, includes two important points of departure in relation to the ninth century iconography. First, the addition of an angel behind Christ's mandorla reflects the popularity, in the West, of the participation of the angelic host in the siege of Hades. Although this theme was familiar to the East, angels are generally absent in the eastern Anastasis. Second, the addition of the combined motif of David and Solomon icono graphically balanced the eighth century examples which primarily demonstrated the will and energy of Christ's divinity. The motif draws attention to Christ's humanity "since the presence of the two kings asserted the historical reality of Christ's human ancestry".[346] The earliest example of the motif of David and Solomon on icons or devotional objects made in the East, appears in the Anastasis image on the Frieschi Morgan Reliquary.

c) Tenth Century
The first compositional type of Anastasis, with the modifications of the ninth century and the amendments of the tenth century, became predominant and was established by the tenth century. Christ's movement towards Adam is either to the right or to the left. Christ holds the scroll in his hand and is usually enclosed in a mandorla of light. Christ lifts an elderly Adam from a shallow sarcophagus, which is mostly included. Eve continues to raise her hands in supplication as she stands more or less ignored behind Adam. The action usually occurs in the topmost part of the underworld. Hades, who is now bound or chained, clings onto Adam. King David and King Solomon are now often included, and John the Baptist is also added. St. John's presence illustrates the fact that at his death he entered Hades to announce to the dead that salvation is at hand, much like he first announced the Saviour on the banks of the Jordan.

---

[344] Kartsonis, *Anastasis*, 231.
[345] Kartsonis, *Anastasis*, 84-85.
[346] Kartsonis, *Anastasis*, 231.

Second Compositional Type

a) Ninth Century

The illustration which accompanies Psalm 67:2 in the Chloudov Psalter is considered to be the earliest surviving eastern example of the second type of Anastasis (see Figure 12.3). Whilst the core of image appears similar to that of the Anastasis in S. Maria Antiqua, there are two noticeable variations. First, the "scene is taking place on the stomach of Hades, who lies on his back irrevocably defeated"[347]. Second, although Christ is facing Adam, Christ's feet give the impression that Christ is moving away from Adam. This miniature and second type of Anastasis, foreshadows the theme of Christ literally dragging Adam out of Hades.

Figure 12.3
Chloudov Psalter

b) Eleventh Century

The second type of Anastasis emerged fully developed in the Phocas Lectionary in the eleventh century. Christ drags Adam out of Hades with one hand and holds a patriarchial cross in the other. Whilst the cross is a reminder of the way in which Christ defeated Hades, and of the suffering of Christ, it functions as "'the royal sceptre' of Christ, whose authority, like that of the rod of Moses, made possible the passage of mankind into a state of grace once more".[348] The cross is almost a weapon that Christ uses against Satan. Paradoxically, the cross as the new symbol

---

[347] Kartsonis, *Anastasis*, 134
[348] Kartsonis, *Anastasis*, 206.

of death, was Satans' weapon. Christ, as victor, uses it against the demon. The topography of the two hills that are divided by the underworld stand "as evidence of the rending of the earth, and the uncovering of the foundation of the world which took place while Christ lay buried in the tomb".[349] The rising Christ personally leads Adam out of the prison of Hades which is shown with its broken doors, keys, bolts and chains. Abel the Shepherd is added to the iconography and stands behind Eve his mother. Although Eve maintains her pleading attitude, Christ still does not seem to acknowledge her existence. The focus of the image is on the triumphant Christ who holds his sceptre-cross and "strides energetically out of Hades against a sea of light".[350]

Third Compositional Type

a) Ninth Century

In the first example of the third type of Anastasis, which accompanies Psalm 81:8 in the Chloudov Psalter, Christ stands fully frontal in a mandorla of light on the head of Hades (see Figure 12.4). Adam and Eve are to the left and right of Christ and are virtually floating in mid-air. Christ raises Adam with his left hand and blesses Eve with his right hand. The symmetry of the composition is compromised by Christ's lifting of Adam.

Figure 12.4
Chloudov Psalter

---

[349] Kartsonis, *Anastasis*, 208.
[350] Kartsonis, *Anastasis*, 213.

b) Eleventh Century

In the Anastasis of Iviron I, the first fully developed example of the third type of Anastasis, "Christ now towers above the trampled figure of Hades, who lies on top of a hill".[351] Adam and Eve, who are to the left and right of Christ at the base of the hill, extend their hands toward Christ, but do not come into contact with him. The symmetry of the composition is reinforced by the spreading of Christ's hands which extend outwards to show the marks of the nails. The two angels above Christ, and the two groups of people above Adam and Eve lifting their hands toward Christ, further enhance the symmetry of the composition.

Fourth Compositional Type

The earliest known examples of the fourth type of Anastasis, a combination of the second and third types, date from the second quarter of the thirteenth century. The fourth type Anastasis fresco in the Church of Christos, Veroia, which was painted during the early fourteenth century, shows Christ hauling Adam out of his sarcophagus while virtually marching away from him (see Figure 12.5). In addition, Christ also pulls Eve by the hand out of her sarcophagus. In so doing Christ raises "for the first time both Adam and Eve, who flank him symmetrically."[352]

Figure 12.5
Church of Christos, Veroia

---

[351] Kartsonis, *Anastasis*, 153.
[352] Kartsonis, *Anastasis*, 9.

A Stylistic Exegesis

Icons can be considered as scripture written in visual imagery[353], and just as we have four canonical gospels to record the events of Jesus' life, since no one account could fully explore the mystery of the incarnation, life death and resurrection of Jesus, so there are sometimes different versions of an event as portrayed in icons. There are, for example, two recognised versions of the icon for the descent of the Holy Spirit. Each version explores more fully a theological aspect of the incident being represented, and it is only by considering all of the icons that we come to a full appreciation of the mystery being made present. In the case of the Anastasis there are four recognised compositional types of the icon. Each of these relate not to the resurrection itself, but to the "Harrowing of Hell". A fifth icon, that of "The Myrrh Bearing Woman", portrays the scriptural account of the resurrection, but it is so different from the harrowing of hell icons that it needs to considered separately. Here we will consider the theology represented by each of the Anastasis icon compositional types.

The first two compositional types of the Anastasis icon are closely related. These show Christ standing on the broken doors of hell with the darkness below filled with the symbols of bondage and enslavement; keys, locks and pieces of chain. In each of them the triumphant Christ holds Adam by the hand and is drawing him out of his sarcophagus. The cross (or a scroll indicating the gospel in early versions) is also prominent. The trampled symbols of death and enslavement, the broken doors of hell, and the drawing out of the sarcophagus, all indicate that these are icons of salvation – salvation won through the cross. However, these two compositional types vary in important respects. First is the relationship of Christ to Adam and the second is the position of the cross.

In the first compositional type (see Figure 12.6), Christ faces Adam and draws him towards himself. The cross is between Adam and Christ so that Adam must come to Christ by passing in front of the cross. This clearly recalls the original *sacramentum*[354] – the oath of allegiance which new legionnaires of Rome gave by passing in front of the standard of the Eagles. Christ is the centre of the icon and the sense of movement in the icon is between Adam and Christ, with Christ drawing Adam towards himself.

---

[353] St. Theodore the Studite quoted in Ouspensky, *Theology of the Icon*, 156.
[354] Cyprian Vagaggini, *Theology and Liturgy in the Fathers- Mysterium and Sacramentum among the Latins*, in *Theological Dimensions of Liturgy* trans. Doyle and Jurgens (Collegeville: Liturgical Press, 1976), 605.

Figure 12.6
The First Compositional Type of the Icon of the Anastasis

This is an icon where salvation has been won and is now offered to Adam. The offer must be accepted by accepting the cross. Here Adam stands for all men. The message is that all need to accept Christ's offer of salvation by accepting the cross. It is, however, Christ who draws man out of death and from the enslavement of sin. The action is His as he draws Adam to himself.

In the second compositional type of this icon (see Figure 12.7) there are two significant differences. The first is that Christ, while still drawing Adam from his sarcophagus, is virtually walking away over the ruins of hell. The second is that the cross is now held up in front of Christ like a standard or a trophy. In this version, Christ does not pull Adam towards himself, but onwards to some other goal towards which he is leading. Once again Roman military references appear. This is very much a triumphal procession with Christ as the conquering victor. The emphasis here is on the salvation of Adam (man) as an achieved fact, and on the call to join in the triumphal procession of Christ into heavenly glory with the cross as the standard. In both of these types the structure and sense of movement is lateral rather than vertical.

Figure 12.7
The second compositional type of icon of the Anastasis in a
mosaic from the Phakis Hosios Lukas Monastery.

In discussing these versions of the icon, some consideration must be given to the position of Eve. She is portayed in much the same way in both compositional types. She stands behind Adam with her veiled hands lifted in entreaty. Her relatively passive presence could be seen as an expression of patriarchal bias, but there is another interpretation. The strong interaction between Adam and Christ can be seen as emphasising Christ as the new Adam. Here is the wonder of the incarnation, where Adam, standing in for all mankind, regards his descendant who not only saves him, but is also his God. In this context, the fact that Eve is depicted at all, shows the determination of the iconographers to demonstrate that all of humanity is included in the salvation of Christ.

The third compositional type of this icon is radically different from the earlier two. It shows Christ in his mandorla, facing to the front with his arms extended. On either side of him are Adam and Eve looking towards Him. The whole icon is quite static with no obvious sense of movement. Christ is in his glory and Adam and Eve, already free from hell, worship him. This icon depicts the fact of the resurrection and the consequent salvation of humanity, rather than its process

At this point it is useful to briefly discuss western imagery of the resurrection with Fra Angelico's famous fresco of the resurrection in the Convento di San Marco, Florence, (see Figure 12.8) as a starting point.

Figure 12.8
Fra Angelico's fresco of the resurrection from the Convent di
San Marco in Florence.

In this beautiful fresco Fra Angelico has combined the third icon compositional type (discussed above) with the icon of the myrrh bearing women. The traditional icon of the myrrh bearing women is very much a representation of the gospel account of the finding of the empty tomb. The tomb is shown as black to indicate that Christ has not only overcome death, but also the darkness of sin. The women are shown approaching the tomb with their jars of ointment, the soldiers guarding the tomb are shown either prostrate in fear or fleeing, and an angel is shown on guard. Significantly, Christ is not really shown in the icon. Following the gospel accounts, the icon does not show the moment of Christ's resurrection, but rather, its immediate aftermath[355]. In combining the two icons, Fra Angelico has produced a painting which speaks powerfully of the fact of the resurrection. Christ carries

---

[355] None of the canonical gospels discuss the moment of resurrection. The only account of it is given in the apocryphal Gospel of Peter.

the standard of his cross in the mandorla of his risen glory, while the women stare at the empty tomb as the angel tells them of the resurrection. This painting is not about salvation. It is about asserting the truth of the resurrection both in the person of the risen Christ and in the "evidence" of the empty tomb. However, Fra Angelico clearly maintains a separation between the two combined elements. Not only are the women and Christ in different portions of the image but there are clouds at the bottom of the mandorla separating Christ from the women. Also, the only interaction between the two elements is the angel who points both at the risen Christ and the empty tomb. The women are unaware of Christ and look either at the angel or at the tomb.

This is a finely composed painting which clearly shows a knowledge and appreciation of eastern iconography[356]. However, it does contain the seeds of future less than desirable developments in western depictions of the resurrection. The first is that the combination of the figure of the risen Christ and the empty tomb has led to attempts to depict the moment of resurrection. These attempts are always aesthetically unfortunate and often verge on the ridiculous. They demonstrate the value of the earlier Christian reticence to depict this moment of the mystery, either in word or image. The second trend is to show Christ in the garden after the resurrection, often in the meeting with Mary. In these images Christ is stripped of his mandorla and appears very much as he would have prior to his passion. The glory of the resurrection is not depicted. Perhaps the worst images are those that combine both trends and show the risen Christ walking out of the tomb as if still bound by the restrictions of time and space. These are images not so much of resurrection as of resuscitation. The deep, reality-changing mystery of the resurrection is reduced to another miraculous display of God's power.

This stripping of the mystery of the resurrection stands in stark opposition to the fourth compositional type and fullest development of the icon of the Anastasis (see Figure 12.9).

---

[356] The composition is so similar to that of the traditional icon of the Dormition of Mary that it is probable Fra Angelico not only knew of the icon but was making a deliberate reference to it.

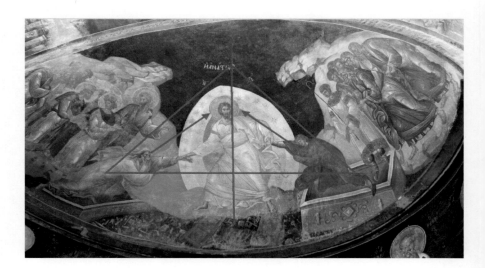

Figure 12.9
The fourth compositional type of the icon of the Anastasis, from a fresco
in the Monastery of the Holy Saviour in the Fields, Constantinople.

Christ in his glorious mandorla, surrounded by stars and standing on the broken gates of hell amid the scattered symbols of sin's enslavement, takes both Adam and Eve by the hand and forcefully draws them out of their tombs. It is a most dynamic image. Christ's knees are bent, but he is not walking in either direction. Rather, the sense of movement is upward. The action is all Christ's. Adam and Eve are being pulled from their tombs towards the Christ and into his mandorla. Significantly, the figure of Christ shows none of the wounds of his passion, but he is shown as the incarnate second person of the Trinity in his full divine glory. The strong sense of upward motion indicates that Adam and Eve are not merely being saved from the enslavement of sin, but are being called, indeed propelled, to something higher. Also, there is a triangular space formed by the figures of Christ, Adam and Eve, a space suggestive of the Triune God. Adam and Eve are being drawn into this space. All of this suggests that this icon is not so much about salvation, but about 'theosis'. Adam and Eve are being drawn into the divine life of the Trinity, divinized by the action of Christ. It is significant that the earlier emphasis on Adam is dispensed with here. Both Adam and Eve are drawn equally into Christ's mandorla emphasising that this divinization is the destiny of all of humanity, indeed of all of creation.

All four of these icons (see Figures 12.6–12.9) show different aspects of the resurrection which is why all four have survived and are still in use. In the first, salvation is offered through the cross. In the second, salvation is achieved and man is led to heaven. In the third, the achieved salvation leads to adoration, and in the fourth, to divinization.

EPILOGUE

IN THE EYES OF GOD

This image of Christ is the most ancient of all portable icons. It was painted by an unknown artist in sixth century Constantinople and its existence is almost a miracle given the upheavals and the destructive forces that swept away its fellows. It was preserved in the remote monastery of St Catherine at Mount Sinai. It is one of only four or five icons that survives the iconoclasts' attentions, and the only one of Christ.

Like people in the realm of the spirit, not all icons are equal. At the very worst an icon may be a mere didactic piece, a routine work of little inspiration. However, some icons are very special indeed because they are true communications with mystery. Even a glance shows that this icon of Christ is no ordinary work. Indeed, it is almost impossible to merely glance at it. Something in the mystery of this work demands our attention and presence.

As sacramental art, icons are designed to focus our prayer by engaging our whole person, body, mind and spirit. How many times have we found ourselves wanting to pray in the midst of the world's noisy chatter, in the midst of the profusion of images of seduction or propaganda? The cares of the world so easily pluck the word of prayer out of our hearts. Our God seems so far away from us, yet the material world with all its stimulations and demands is so close. We have nothing upon which to focus our attention, no anchor to our mind, no centre for our hearts and no rest for our senses. It is here that the icon comes to help us safeguard the inner space where we can keep our eyes upon the Lord.

Icons are meant to be gazed upon. Through devout gaze they come to engrave themselves upon the mind and enter the heart. If we stay present to an icon, such as this most ancient icon of the Lord, it begins to communicate a stillness and a presence within us that can guide us in good times and bad, that is present to us in our decision-making, in our speaking, in our work and simple pleasures and relationships.

Words fail to describe the deep and mysterious gaze of the Christ. When the gaze of Christ first comes upon us we inevitably feel exposed, even as Peter was when the Lord "*turned and looked straight at him*" (Lk 22:61) in the midst of his denials. The Lord's gaze bestows the grace of repentance and conversion more surely than all the emotional compulsion of "born again" revivalism. These eyes are not severe, nor do they condemn, but certainly they confront and expose all that is false in us. Confronted by this gaze, we can only pray, "*O where can I go from your spirit, where can I flee from your face?*" (Ps 139:7).

Far from exciting shame or fear, such as to provoke rebellion or hypocrisy, the eyes of the Christ expose us to our radical weakness and poverty. They invite us not to flee away, but to flee to him, within him. As Henri Nouwen has remarked, "*They are the eyes of God, who sees us in our most hidden places and loves us with a divine mercy.*"[357]

---

[357] Henri Nouwen, *Behold the Beauty of the Lord: Praying with Icons* (Notre Dame, Ind.: Ave Maria Press, 1987), 52-54.

BIBLIOGRAPHY

Baggley, J. *Doors of Perception: Icons and their Spiritual Significance*. London: Mowbray, 1987.

Barrow, G. "The Iconoclastic Crisis" www.orthodoxresearchinstitute.org/articles/ church_history/barrow_iconoclastic_crisis.htm [accessed 12 August 2004].

Belting, Hans. *Likeness and Presence: A History of the Image Before the Era of Art*. Translated by Edmund Jephcott. Chicago: University of Chicago Press, 1997.

Bigham, Steven. *The Image of God the Father in Orthodox Theology and Iconography and Other Studies*. Torrance CA: Oakwood Publications, 1995.

Bradley, I. *Celtic Christian Communities: Live the Tradition*. Kelowna, British Columbia, Canada: Northstone Publishing, 2000.

Brentnall, J. "The Language of Orthodox Icons: A Resource For Teachers Of Religious Education" http://www.farmington.ac.uk/documents/old_docs/ Brentnall.htm [accessed 12 August 2004].

Bur, J. *How to Understand the Virgin Mary*. New York: Continuum, 1996.

Byzantine Melkite Euchologion. Jounieh Lebanon: St Paul's Printing Press, 1972.

Cahill, T. *How the Irish Saved Civilisation: The Untold Story of Ireland's Heroic Role from the Fall of Rome to the Rise of Medieval Europe*. London: Hodder and Stoughton, 1995.

Charlesworth, J, trans. *The Odes of Solomon* http://www.misericordia.edu/users/ davies/thomas.odes.htm [accessed 14 June 2005].

Collins, Gregory. *The Glenstal Book of Icons: Praying with the Glenstal Icons*. Dublin: Columba Press, 2002.

Corrigan, K. "Book Review". *The Art Bulletin*. 71, no. 2 (1989): 312.

Cross, Lawrence. *Eastern Christianity: The Byzantine Tradition*, rev. ed. Virginia: Eastern Christian Publications, 1999.

Cunningham, Mary. *Faith in the Byzantine World*. Oxford: Lion Publishing, 2002.

"The Mother of God in Early Byzantine Homilies". *Sobornost* 10.2 (1988): 53-67.

Damascene, John. *Apologia of St John Damascene Against Those Who Decry Holy Images* http://www.balamand.edu.lb/iob/theology/Joicons1.htm [accessed 8 August 2004].

Davis, L. *The First Seven Ecumenical Councils (325-787): Their History and Theology*. Wilmington, Delaware: Michael Glazier, 1987.

Dragas, G. "St John Damascene's Teaching about the Holy Icons." In *Icons: Windows on Eternity*, edited by G. Limouris, 53-72. Geneva: WCC Publications, 1990.

Understanding the Resurrection through Christ's Descent into Hades http:// www.orthodoxnews.netfirms.com/170/Understanding%20the%20 Resurrection.htm [accessed 23 June 2005].

Elsner, Jas. *Art and the Roman Viewer: The Transformation of Art from the Pagan World to Christianity*. Cambridge: Cambridge University Press, 1995.

Evdokimov, Michael. *Light from the East: Icons in Liturgy and Prayer*. New York: Paulist Press, 2004.

Evdokimov, Paul. *The Art of the Icon: A Theology of Beauty*. California: Oakwood, 1992.

"Feast of the Annunciation of Our Most Holy Lady, the Theotokos and Ever Virgin Mary" http://www.goarch.org/en/special/listen_learn_share/ annunciation/learn/index.asp?pri [accessed 15 November2004].

"Feast of the Entrance into the Temple of Our Most Holy Lady the Theotokos"

http://www.goarch.org/en/special/listen_learn_share/vmpresentation/ learn/ [accessed 21 October 2004].

Forest, Jim. *Praying With Icons*. Maryknoll New York: Orbis Books, 2002.

Gerhard, H. *The World of Icons*. London: John Murray, 1971.

Great and Holy Saturday Matins

http://www.ocf.org/OrthodoxPage/prayers/triodion/hwk_sat [accessed 16 June 2005].

Harries, Richard. *Art and the Beauty of God: A Christian Understanding*. London: Mowbray, 1993.

Hickey, D. "Dormition of the Virgin". In *New Catholic Encyclopedia*, 2nd ed. (2003), 4: 875-876.

"Images of the Theotokos in Byzantine Iconography" http://www.msu. edu/~rabbatjo/entrancetemple.htm [accessed 24 October, 2004].

James, M. *The Apocryphal New Testament*. Oxford: Clarendon, 1955.

James Montague Rhodes, *The Apocryphal New Testament* (London: Oxford University Press, 1924, 1955.

Joyce T. *Celtic Christianity: Sacred Tradition, a Vision of Hope*. Maryknoll NY: Orbis Books, 1998.

Kartsonis, A.D. *Anastasis: The Making of an Image*. Princeton, New Jersey: Princeton University Press, 1986.

Kelly, J. "Heresy/Heretics". In *The Modern Catholic Encyclopedia*. Revised and Expanded Edition. (2004), 354-357.

Langlinais, J. "Assumption of Mary". In *New Catholic Encyclopedia*, 2nd ed. (2003), 1: 797-801.

Limouris, G. "Introductory Note". In *Icons. Windows on Eternity,* edited by G.Limouris, ix-x. Geneva: WCC Publications, 1990.

"The Microcosm and Macrocosm of the Icon: Theology, Spirituality and Worship in Colour." In *Icons Windows on Eternity*, edited by G. Limouris, 93-123. Geneva:WCC Publications, 1990.

"March 2012 Prayer and Reflection" http://www.catholicdigest.com/articles/food_ fun/catholic_art/2012/02-15/march-2012-prayer-and-reflection [accessed 1 November, 2012].

Matusiak, J. "Entrance of the Mother of God into the Temple" http://www.oca. org/pages/orth_chri/Q-and-A_OLD/Entrance-into-the=Temple.html [accessed 24 October 2004].

Mauriello, M. "November 21: Presentation of Mary" http://www.udayton.edu/ mary/meditations/Nov21.html [accessed 5 October 2004].

Mileant, A. "The Feast of Annunciation: The Beginning of Our Salvation". Translated by A. Perede http://www.fatheralexander.org/booklets/ english/blagov_e.htm [accessed 15 November, 2004].

Mother Mary and Archimandrite Kallistos Ware, trans. *The Festal Menaion* (London: Faber and Faber, 1969.

Muretov, Dimitri "Homily". *Journal of the Moscow Patriarchate*, 14 (1984): 28-29.

Nes, Solrunn. *The Mystical Language of Icons*. London: St Pauls, 2000.

Nouwen, Henri J.M. *Behold The Beauty Of The Lord: Praying With Icons*, Notre Dame, Ind.: Ave Maria Press, 1987.

Onasch, Konrad, and Annemarie Schnieper, *Icons: The Fascination and the Reality*. Translated by D.G.Conklin. New York: Riverside Book Company, Inc. 1995.

Ouspensky, Leonide *Theology of the Icon*. Crestwood NY: St Vladimir's Seminary Press, 1978.

"Iconography of the Descent of the Holy Spirit". *St Vladimir's Theological Quarterly*, 31 (1987): 309-347.

Ouspensky, Leonide, and Vladimir Lossky. *The Meaning of Icons*. Crestwood NY: St Vladimir's Seminary Press, 1989.

Parry, K. "Dormition". In *The Blackwell Dictionary of Eastern Christianity*, edited by Ken Parry, David Melling, Dimitri Brady, Sidney Griffith, and John Healey, 165. Oxford, UK: Blackwell Publishers, 2000.

"John of Damascus". In *The Blackwell Dictionary of Eastern Christianity*,

edited by Ken Parry, David Melling, Dimitri Brady, Sidney Griffith, and John Healey, 270-271. Oxford, UK: Blackwell Publishers, 2000.

"Nativity of the Mother of God." In *The Blackwell Dictionary of Eastern Christianity*, edited by Ken Parry, David Melling, Dimitri Brady, Sidney Griffith, and John Healey, 338-339. Oxford, UK: Blackwell Publishers, 2000.

Pelikan, Jaroslav. *Imago Dei The Byzantine Apologia for Icons*. New Haven and London: Yale University Press, 1990.

Percival, H.R., trans. *The Seven Ecumenical Councils of the Undivided Church*. Vol 14 of *Nicene and Post-Nicene Fathers*, 2nd Series, edited by Philip Schaff and Henry Wace. Grand Rapids MI: W.B.Eerdmans, 1955.

Quenot, Michel. *The Icon: Window on the Kingdom*. New York: St Vladimir's Seminary Press, 1996.

Ramos-Poqui, Guillem. *The Technique of Icon Painting*. Tunbridge Wells, UK: Burns & Oates, 1990.

Raya, Joseph, and Baron Jose De Vinck. *Byzantine Daily Worship*. Allendale, N.J.: Alleluia Press, 1969.

Ritchey, M. "The Icon of the Annunciation" http://www.melkite.org/Mediation3. html [accessed 16 November 2004].

Roberts, Alexander, and James Donaldson. *St. Ignatius of Antioch to the Trallians*

http://www.earlychristianwritings.com/text/ignatius-trallians-longer.html [accessed 17 June 2005].

Sahas, Daniel. *Icons and Logos: Sources in Eighth-Century Iconoclasm*. Toronto: University of Toronto Press, 1986.

Scouteris, C. "Never as Gods: Icons and their Veneration" http://www. orthodoxresearchinstitute.org/articles/scouteris_icons.htm [accessed 7 September 2004].

Shannon, William H. (Ed.). *The Hidden Ground of Love: The Letters of Thomas Merton on Religious Experience and Social Concerns*. New York: Farrar, Straus & Giroux, 1985.

Stead, Dom Julian. *The Church, the Liturgy and the Soul of Man: The Mystagogia of St Maximus the Confessor.* Still River, MA: St Bede's Publications, 1982.

Stuart, John. *Ikons*. London: Faber & Faber, 1975.

"St Melito of Sardis" http://www.catholic-forum.com/saints/saintm18.htm [accessed 30 June2005].

Synaxarion of the Lenten Triodion and Pentecostarion. Edited by David Kidd and Gabriella Ursache. Rives Junction, MI: HDM, 1999.

The Columbia Electronic Encyclopaedia, 6th ed. Columbia University Press, 2004.

"The Blessing and Hallowing of Icons" http://www.goach.org/en/chapel/ liturgical_texts/icon_blessing.asp [accessed 16 September, 2004].

"The Nativity of the Blessed Virgin Mary" http://www.byzantines.net/ SaintAthanasius/tract58.htm [accessed 2 October 2004].

The Protevangelion http://www.pseudepigrapha.com/LostBooks/protevangelion. htm [accessed 3 October 2004].

"The Veneration of Icons in the Tradition of the Byzantine Rite" http://www. byzantines.net/moreinfo/venerateIcons.htm [accessed 12 August 2004].

Thompson, R.W., trans. *De Incarnatione*. Edited by R.W.Thompson. Oxford; Oxford University Press, 1971.

Turner, D. "Iconoclasm". In *The Blackwell Dictionary of Eastern Christianity*,

edited by Ken Parry, David Melling, Dimitri Brady, Sidney Griffith, and John Healey, 239-242. Oxford, UK: Blackwell Publishers, 2000.

Turpa, G. "Icons: Aids in Spiritual Struggle" http://www.stuladimis.ca/library/ icons-spiritual-struggle.htm [accessed 7 September 2004].

Vagaggini, Cyprian. *Theological Dimensions of Liturgy,* translated by Doyle and Jurgens. Collegeville: Liturgical Press, 1976.

Von Rad, Gerhard. *Old Testament Theology*. Vol.1. Edinburgh: Oliver and Boyd, 1962.

Von Schönborn, Christoph. *God's Human Face: The Christ- Icon*. San Francisco: Ignatius Press, 1994.

Williams, Rowan. *The Dwelling of the Light: Praying with Icons of Christ*. Mulgrave, Vic.: John Garratt Publishing, 2003.